"For all those seeking integration between doctrine and life, Demkovich's soul-centered spirituality provides a key. Spirituality animates doctrine, which in turn gives meaning to life. An animating spirituality requires religious commitment to beliefs and a community that embodies them. At a time when spiritualities proliferate, and we may not know which way to turn, Demkovich's approach is both grounded and life-giving."

> — Donald Goergen, OP
> St. Dominic Priory, St. Louis, Missouri
> Author of *Sexual Celibate* and *Fire of Love: Encountering the Holy Spirit*

"People often declare, 'I'm spiritual but not religious.' Yet as Michael Demkovich so convincingly argues in his wise and erudite new book, *A Soul-Centered Life*, spirituality not grounded in religious community nor firmly tethered to solid doctrine fails to deliver, for ultimately it cannot address the great questions of life. Packed to overflowing with theological and historical riches, Demkovich's book takes its stand against private, self-pleasing spiritualities and points the way toward a fully integrated, deeply meaningful, intellectually satisfying Christian life."

> — Paula Huston
> Author of *Forgiveness: Following Jesus into Radical Loving*

A Soul-Centered Life

Exploring an Animated Spirituality

Michael Demkovich, OP

A Michael Glazier Book

LITURGICAL PRESS

Collegeville, Minnesota

www.litpress.org

A Michael Glazier Book published by Liturgical Press.

Cover design by Ann Blattner. Photo courtesy of Photos.com.

Excerpts from *Ignatius of Loyola: Spiritual Exercises and Selected Works* (*CWS*; Edited by George E. Ganss, SJ). Copyright © 1991 by George E. Ganss, SJ. Paulist Press, Inc., New York/Mahwah, NJ. Reprinted by permission of Paulist Press, Inc. www.paulistpress.com.

1   2   3   4   5   6   7   8   9

Library of Congress Cataloging-in-Publication Data

Demkovich, Michael.
    A soul-centered life : exploring an animated spirituality / Michael Demkovich.
        p. cm.
    Includes index.
    ISBN 978-0-8146-5512-2 — ISBN 978-0-8146-5728-7 (e-book)
        1. Spirituality.   I. Title.

BV4501.3.D455 2010
248—dc22
                                                                2009053721

Contents

Introduction

Something is missing! Something that I feel should be part of my life but it just isn't there! Something keeps gnawing at me and I can't figure it out! Something is missing in me and I wish I knew what it was! Something, but what? These words echo what I have heard from various people in spiritual direction and what I have heard in my own heart. These haunting hungers hit us all. Like the pangs of a person deprived of food, we long for something to satisfy the void in us. This spiritual hunger keeps us looking, longing for the thing that fills us, makes us complete. Sadly, many of us end up looking in the wrong places and gorge ourselves with unhealthy things like self-centeredness, or addictions, or superficiality. And still we continue to find that something is missing, something so amazingly fulfilling that we are still left hungering for its bountiful harvest. This hunger arises from the very soul of a person and it longs to be filled. A woman who has spent her life working with this world's neglected said, "There is more hunger in the world for love and appreciation than for bread." She knew the soul's real longing. She was Mother Teresa.

One of the great blessings in my ministry has been the special invitation to enter into the sacred ground of another human being, to be able to spend time on the spiritual journey with another person who has very often traveled many different roads. Another part of my life that I hold as a blessing has been the opportunity to study the Catholic tradition and to share this with others. Both of these aspects seem to complement one another, and I have come to see how theological is the spiritual life, and how spiritual is genuine theology. Mother Teresa was talking about a spiritual hunger, and the only way to feed such hunger is to learn the lessons of those who know where this food is to be found. Why would a wealthy person with political privilege and a promising career leave all these things for the simplicity of a life as a monk? Why would a person who was safe in the quiet comfort of prayer be moved to insert herself into the political struggles of her day? Why would a soldier face his debilitating wounds and reject its bitterness, surrendering his own will to God? Why would a religious woman, teaching in a posh school, reject the obedience her vows prescribed and set out to live a life of destitution? We meet these questions when we encounter people like Maximus the Confessor, Catherine of Siena, Ignatius of Loyola, and Mother Teresa of Calcutta. There is something to be found in people like these that make their lives so meaningful, so desirable. They can teach us what a truly animating spirituality is meant to be.

For many of us, spirituality is a topic that conjures up all sorts of ideas, both sublime and silly. Spirituality books are shelved in stores under headings like the occult, or self-help, or religion, or New Age. It is difficult to find a common definition among authors or even among religious people. So one might ask, why another book on spirituality?

My interest was born out of attempting to live the reality and trying to teach it to others. The challenge is finding that perfect balance between knowing and being. So many books come close, but they just don't capture what so many of us desire. In 1997 I was given a challenging task: to teach Christian spirituality at Blackfriars in Oxford to brilliant and critical students. Being trained as a theologian and having years of doing spiritual direction, I knew that a survey course just wouldn't be enough. The past decade has afforded me time and opportunity to develop some thoughts, research key questions, and formulate an approach to spirituality that makes sense both intellectually and emotionally, both to the head and to the heart.

This work explores the study of spirituality from the perspective of integrating faith and life, bringing together that something more the soul desires. These two dimensions are met time and time again in all the great spiritual writers in the Christian tradition, and others as well. It is difficult to comprehend spirituality outside of its tradition, its formative environment. Doctrine and a person's life weave a fabric that is rich in texture, color, and strength. This unique integration is what most fascinates me in the spiritual writers. At the same time I noticed a flaw in the study of spirituality. Many approaches struck me as too uncritical; they avoid identifying a standard for spirituality, some guide to help the student ask about a spirituality's worth. This shortcoming has given rise to what I would call a tourist's approach to spirituality. The package deal looks at a list of favorite writers, a survey of the greats. But they never really tell us why! What is it in these writers that makes their spiritual insights of value? Or, on the other hand, what dangers might be present in pursuing a particular spirituality that doesn't suit a person?

Indeed something is missing if we think that spirituality is only meant for a few special people. Something is missing if we approach spirituality without asking it to answer tough questions or without expecting it to be genuinely satisfying. Something is missing if we expect that the lessons that animate spirituality are easily had, demanding them to conform to the limits of our own ideas and not struggling to allow ourselves to be transformed. Something will be missing if our criterion is our own comfort and coziness, choosing not to face the challenges that really change us. If you find that something is missing in the very soul of your being, then, I am certain that this book has something for you.

Learning the really meaningful and satisfying lessons of life requires study, our being students once more. Interestingly these words come from the Latin root *studere*, which means "to take pains, to strive after, to be eager." One can't really study spirituality without any effort, and though I wish I could share these lessons with the wave of my hand, we all know that learning requires effort. So, I find that on such journeys of learning it is always helpful to map out what lies ahead.

Part 1 presents a critical overview of the current approaches to spirituality, a kind of status report or *status quaestionis*. I want to warn the reader in advance that this part is challenging but necessarily so. Once you get part 1, the rest of the book falls into place. It is like the skeleton key that grants access to all the locked doors. This integrative and animating approach gives the reader tools for understanding spirituality. There are three factors developed in part 1 that require a deeper understanding in order to genuinely study spirituality. I want to state that this is not to take away from the devotional and inspirational ways in which spiritual writings touch countless people, but it is to examine these writings and writers with a critical eye. The three factors presented in part 1 are the self (a person's sense of integrity and transcendence), life (one's view of the world and understanding of humanity), and doctrine (one's belief about creation and redemption). These factors create a dynamic approach to spirituality that sees it as an animating ground for doing and living theology. This can be called a *locus theologicus*, a place where theology takes shape, where one's encounter with the divine finds expression. As I said, this is the most challenging part of the book, but the most essential to appreciating the rest of the book.

Part 2 examines four spiritual ways that help us study spirituality. The first two ways (asceticism and mysticism) are familiar to most students of spirituality. The remaining two (aesthetic and social-critical) reflect a modern encounter with post-Reformation forms of spirituality. The traditional studies of spirituality focused on the historical development of these first three ways and not the social-critical approach. In our critical encounter we see the textual and contextual dynamic that makes these spiritualities timeless, how the written word and lived reality make life meaningful. While history has shown us these approaches, the way the sun illuminates different realities as its light falls differently during the day, a critical reading discloses their context that is hidden amid the historical circumstances. For example, asceticism can't be limited to the early desert monks or those who try to imitate their lives. No, asceticism, as an animating spirituality, is meaningful and satisfying because of the particular weave of factors. It bestows a sense of the person's place in the cosmos and one's human purpose, a conviction about creation itself and ultimate happiness. These factors animate asceticism, as well as mysticism and the others. We might ask if all of these have always been, but has history just kept them waiting offstage until they heard their cue? Are there emerging spiritualities even now that we fail to notice? The answer to such questions will be found in our critically meeting the spiritual geniuses of our day, looking to see how they achieve spiritual integration. In examining these factors, in seeking them at work in a person, spirituality's scope is broadened. By engaging the animating dynamics of spirituality we appreciate the person, one's life, and one's embracing the theological task. A rich doctrinal tradition like Catholicism affords a vibrant way of integrating spirituality. Catholic doctrines have well served countless men and women to integrate their lives, integrating faith and life in an animating spirituality. This look at the context of spiritual writers and the formative doctrines that shape spirituality provides the critical tools for understanding a spiritual writer and his or her particular spirituality.

Part 3 puts forth my conclusion and reflections on a critical study of spirituality in its theological and moral aspects, a life that is meaningful and satisfying. I have come to see through this approach that there is a pastoral bonus. It enables one to meet the parishioner, the person in spiritual direction, or the would-be disciple of a spiritual master with critical care to that person's own unique needs. An addict, or scientist, or artist, or activist may all long for a spiritual home, but not all in the same way. By approaching spirituality in this animating way, one is more aware of matching a person and his or her life context to a spiritual tradition that offers this person greater satisfaction and meaning in life. It also means being able to help a person who has gotten into an unhealthy spirituality to find the tools and use them to evaluate the situation. It asks questions about a particular spirituality's suitability or appropriateness for the life of a specific person and context.

There really is something more to life, and spirituality meets the mystery of this something more. The study of spirituality has been a lifelong fascination for me. My hope is that you find in this approach something truly animating, something that allows you to meet the spiritual writers and sense the integrity of their reality. I hope that it helps you to see in your life a place where you can encounter the divine and seek to express that reality in ways that are intellectually meaningful and morally satisfying, making life something more, and nothing less than what it is called to be.

* * *

I am grateful to the people in my life who have shared with me their spiritual journey, who taught me by their example of life and by their words of wisdom. I am especially grateful for my students. Their questions and conversations on spirituality have helped me to see how important personal integration is in human life, and yet they desire to belong to a tradition of faith that guides them. Over the years this book has taken different forms, and for all those who helped me in this process I am grateful. I am very appreciative of the help given by Mrs. Joan See and Mr. Dennis Kane in reading over the various drafts for clarity and corrections. I also would like to thank Ms. Anna Walenski and Mr. Andrew Radespiel for their help in indexing this work. Finally, I wish to thank Liturgical Press and Hans Christoffersen and all the individuals who saw this work to publication.

Part I

Understanding Spirituality

The wonderful beauty of the Church's teaching on this abiding presence of the Holy Spirit, while it deepens our acquaintance with His mysterious governance of the universe and discovers to us the hidden beauties of our soul's life, should bring also its measure of comfort, for whatever makes us conscious of the intimacy of God's dealing with us lessens life's greatest trouble, its loneliness.

Bede Jarrett, O.P.
The Abiding Presence of the Holy Ghost (1918)

Chapter One

Challenges

"Spirituality" is not an easy topic to study! There is an ever changing sea of issues and interests. Very often people embrace a particular practice without realizing the full implications. Spirituality has become the umbrella term for everything from Tridentine Masses to occult practices. Retreat houses serve up a blend of religion-lite, New Age thought, and primitive religious rituals. Most people are quite content with this cocktail of self-help and personal empowerment, only to lament their hangover of hollow rituals and superficial concerns.

But what if they are right? What if spirituality really is about personal fulfillment and actualization? For many people, isn't this the purpose of spirituality? While it provides them with a sense of personal transcendence, I fear it lacks the challenge of self-transcendence. This can be demonstrated in two different kinds of relationships common among people. One relationship is the one you might have with a lifelong friend; the other the relationship you may have with your pet dog, cat, or iguana. In the first one a true friend challenges us, calls something forth from within us, demands of us change, genuine growth, and human flourishing. In the second relationship, with our pets, we see that they are there for us. Our pets are an extension of our own needs, to feed or bathe or care for as we see fit. No pet is going to tell us to quit smoking, or end an abusive relationship, or lose thirty pounds. Fortunately, genuine spirituality is about true friendship. Sadly, for some people it is spirituality as their "pets."

This happens because people all too often inadvertently reduce spirituality to the private possession of an individual, and so it loses its communal dimension. The question of whose spirituality (Francis, Ignatius, or Benedict) creates a false sense that spirituality is personal and private. Nothing could be further from the truth. The great traditions of spiritual writers are not about individual quirkiness. In fact, it is about community—a community that is gathered around the religious tradition, made alive in very real people called disciples. If spirituality is reduced to merely reading texts of a historical person, a very vital dimension is left out. That dimension is spirituality's ability to constitute a community that shares this spiritual vision, a vision that touches the very souls of women and men who believe.

Fortunately, I came across the short work by the Dominican Bede Jarrett titled *The Abiding Presence of the Holy Ghost*. Immediately I felt I had found someone who shared my concern—the presence of God in the depth of human existence, called the soul. The soul has been discarded and seen as unmarketable, yet it is what desperately needs to be restored.

> Thus we say God is more in a man's soul than anywhere else in creation, since in man's soul God is more perfectly expressed. It is therefore with great reverence that I should regard all creation, but with especial reverence that I should look to the dignity of every human soul.[1]

Consequently, one is challenged to approach spirituality using the doctrine of the soul as the key to unlocking its meaning. In

[1] Bede Jarrett, *The Abiding Presence of the Holy Ghost* (London: Burns, Oates & Washbourne, Ltd., 1918, 2nd ed. 1935) 4.

so doing we will see how spirituality is one aspect of the deepest religious desire for human flourishing.

Perspectives on Spirituality

To the east of Albuquerque, where I live, stands a mountain range known for its sheer facade and whitish stone that is transformed by the setting sun into shades of pink, then red. The Spanish settlers called these mountains the Sandias, or watermelon, due to this coloring effect like that of a ripening watermelon. To the north these same mountains are seen by the Pueblo Indians and are called by a different name. They see the western face and a lower ridge as well as the mountains' long sloping eastern side, which resembles the shell of a turtle, with its head facing west. They call it the Sacred Turtle Mountains. Our perspective on the very same object can mean very different things given our community and interpretation. Our perspective on spirituality is no different, and the literature reflects this.

While many studies exist on the topic of spirituality, few approach the topic from the perspective of genuine religious formation of the human person. Formation takes place within a community of faith. Often the emphasis is placed on subjective criteria for spirituality, what it does for me. This neglects two important aspects of spirituality: (1) the role of mentors, and (2) the sense of belonging. Each name given to the mountains teaches the community and establishes the bonds of the community. These two aspects can further be understood as doctrinal and social aspects of a genuine Christian spirituality. Consequently, I wish to devote special attention to this doctrinal and social integration that is at the heart of spiritual life.

In the study of spirituality an important starting point is the language used for the spiritual life. Given the great range of discourse found in both historical and psychological studies on the subject, one has to ask what is meant by the terms used to discuss the spiritual life. How are we to look at the mountains? How do we look at spirituality? Several works serve to illustrate the difficulties that face our looking at spirituality. The first two

are collected essays intended to study spirituality—one from
the perspective of worship, the other from that of the academy.
The Study of Spirituality was published by Oxford University
Press in 1986 and was widely used in courses on spirituality.
Modern Christian Spirituality was put out by Scholars Press in
1990 and attempted to examine spirituality as an academic
discipline. A third book is the 1991 work by Philip Sheldrake
titled *Spirituality & History: Questions of Interpretation and Method*,
revised in 1995.[2] All three works provide a status report and
illustrate different looks at spirituality, from the perspective of
liturgy, the academy, and history.

Spirituality as Liturgy

It makes good sense to treat spirituality as liturgy, and the 1986
work edited by Cheslyn Jones and others is instructive. It has
become a basic text for many courses on spirituality, following
the earlier volume titled *The Study of Liturgy* (1978). It attempts
to theologically introduce the historical exposition of spirituality.
This effort is found in part 2 of the book and is conveniently
grouped according to "schools." The entire work concludes with
a treatment of some pastoral applications in part 3. However,
it is at the close of this work's preface that the editors have
furnished some comment on the term "spirituality." While the
liturgical point of their departure indicates the influence of
seventeenth-century English Caroline Divines like John Donne,
it also favors the clerical realities of the French school.[3] The edi-

---

[2] Cheslyn Jones, Geoffrey Wainwright, and Edward Yarnold, eds., *The Study of Spirituality* (New York: Oxford University Press, 1986). Bradley C. Hanson, ed., *Modern Christian Spirituality: Methodological and Historical Essays* (Atlanta, GA: Scholars Press, 1990). Philip Sheldrake, *Spirituality & History: Questions of Interpretation and Method* (London: SPCK, 1991, 1995 rev.).

[3] The French school may be roughly dated from the seventeenth century and was strongly influenced by clerical realities—liturgical life (the sacraments and Holy Eucharist). It was important in defining the spiritual life for the past two centuries, as can be seen in the great French contribution in the *Dictionnaire de Spiritualité*.

tors have suggested that their interest rose in reaction to the critical thought (modern scientific analysis) of Victorian Protestantism. In the Anglo-Saxon world a desire for "religious experience" emerged to counter the analytical thought of the modern world. It is exactly here that the editors tip their hand, referring to such "religious practices" in terms of St. Augustine's formula *lex orandi, lex credendi* (or to paraphrase, how we pray dictates what we believe). This innocent comment reveals their governing assumption: spirituality is linked to liturgy (Jones, xxv). A look at their arguments is helpful in our study of spirituality.

The theological introduction to spirituality, which comprises part 1 of this work, similarly stresses this link to liturgy. Jones' two contributions first showcase the "common prayer-private devotion" axis with a creedal interpretation of common worship. His hope in "Liturgy and Personal Devotion" (3–9) is to prove that individual worship (i.e., spirituality) adheres to canons similar to those of liturgy (albeit scaled to the individual). Individual worship is seen as the equivalent of spirituality, so that the primary way of looking at spirituality is to be found in liturgy. His second article, "Mysticism, Human and Divine" (17–24), sees religious mystical experience as a "general capacity of the human spirit" (23), which is conditioned or qualified by one's religious (liturgical) tradition. I agree that there is this desire of the human spirit to be satisfied only out of the context of a particular religious tradition. However, we must be careful not to too narrowly define this religious tradition in "liturgical" terms. While the liturgical life and prayer of the Christian community is extremely valuable, I am a bit suspicious of the use of liturgical worship in understanding spirituality. The danger, although a subtle danger, is to establish a false criterion drawn from liturgy in determining the validity of any particular spirituality. In other words, if a spiritual practice doesn't fit into the norms of liturgical celebration (e.g., painting or walking), it will be overlooked as not being truly spiritual (e.g., spiritualities of praxis or of liberation). Such a danger seems to be present in Jones' treatment of spirituality under the narrow aesthetics of "nature, art, and the inter-personal" (22–23).

Certainly the liturgy is something more than defined rubrics and set rituals; its aesthetical aspect clearly shapes our understanding of spirituality. But I find Edward Yarnold's contribution to *The Study of Spirituality* suffers from the same difficulty as his coeditor in attempting to offer a "Theology of Christian Spirituality" (9–17). Yarnold starts by rendering too uncritically Geoffrey Wainwright's "combination of praying and living" (9) to simply define spirituality as the combination of praise and liturgy.[4] Furthermore, Yarnold (in his chapter titled "The Media of Spirituality," 39–44) pays single tribute to the aesthetics of liturgy (place, architecture, apparel, ceremony, music). However, realize that when one defines reality aesthetically, beauty becomes the rule that holds us to its measure. The error is to think that aesthetic correctness means theological correctness. This begs the question of ugly spiritualities. Is it possible to have a nine-to-five spirituality that deals with the mundane realities of life? It seems that apart from liturgy, Yarnold offers brief attention to Scriptures, ecclesial life, as well as the link between action and contemplation. In fact, a more critical reading of pages 42–44 reveals that even these elements, Scripture and ecclesial life, are taken as no more than refractions of liturgical worship.

Looking at spirituality as liturgy poses some problems. However, this is not to say that the fundamental premise of *The Study of Spirituality* is false, or to be discarded. Clearly it is an orthodox premise to maintain that liturgy and spirituality remain tethered by the *lex orandi, lex credendi* formula of the Christian tradition. However, the fuller doctrinal body of the Christian ensemble suggests that such a reading runs the risk of eclipsing the nonliturgical character of spirituality. One needs to question whether truly Catholic spirituality ("catholic" in the broadest sense) does not also contain a moral imperative that demands an ascetical hermeneutic as well as an aesthetical one. This affords us a broader language for studying the spiritual life. It is not only

[4] Wainwright will later use Richard Neibuhr's typologies in treating "Types of Spirituality," which is the final chapter (pp. 592–605).

the medieval transcendent or the modern aesthetic of "beauty" but also the ethical notion of the good, the moral good that defines spirituality. Is there something within the Catholic tradition that guarantees the nonliturgical praxis of spirituality?

Perhaps if we focus less on the ritual aspects and more on the prayer aspect in the liturgy, we will safeguard the liturgical approach. It is in light of this concern that the Ulanovs (Ann and Barry), in their chapter "Prayer and Personality: Prayer as Primary Speech" (24–33), offer a better paradigm for defining spirituality. They do this by treating honest prayer as primary speech. Their argument is based on the concept of "truth of consciousness" (26) as developed by R. G. Collingwood.[5] True consciousness, in this sense, implies frank and honest self-acknowledgment of one's true feelings. "Primary speech" would be such a true consciousness applied to one's discourse with God in prayer. It is speech at its truest and most elemental level of discourse. One might say it is speaking from one's soul. In their chapter the Ulanovs open our understanding of spirituality to the inner depth of the person, the classic *locus theologicus* of spiritual theology, the human soul. While their closing illustration is an application of primary speech to liturgical worship as the principle for confrontation with "true consciousness," the weight of their argument also allows us to insert any aspect of genuine human life (such as one's job, play, and lifestyle) instead of liturgy in understanding spirituality. "Primary speech" allows a fuller sense of spirituality.

The chapter by Anthony Russell in this 1986 work on "Sociology and the Study of Spirituality" (33–38) illustrates the inherent difficulty surrounding a scientific study of spirituality. However, it is important to note that Russell errs in his analysis of "knowledge" in Western society. He fails to observe that his critique is more correctly directed at modern Enlightenment's distinction "between knowledge as that which can be apprehended and

---

[5] R. G. Collingwood, *The Principles of Art* (Oxford: Clarendon Press, 1955/ New York: OUP, 1958) 216, 287, 291.

verified by individuals for themselves and mere opinion" (34).
This need for clear and distinct ideas is the real historical culprit
for banishing those "matters of the heart" from the respectability
afforded the intellect that Russell laments. Consequently, he
distinguishes two forms of spirituality, one "ecclesial," the other
"privatized." In doing so he sees two classes: (1) the "clerical-
priestly" and (2) the "lay-popularist" types. This is due to a need
for Cartesian clarity in distinguishing along intellectual/non-
intellectual terms. Discussion prior to Descartes, which Russell
overlooks and is still present in contemporary Catholic spirituality, is the reality of the soul's two powers to love and to know,
or in scholastic terms, the will and the intellect. Russell's article
casts the reader outside Jones' liturgical typology, far beyond
the insights of the Ulanovs' "primary speech" typology, into the
crisis of modern scientific analysis of spirituality. Now we are
forced to ask after the proper methodology to be used in understanding Christian spirituality, and our next book does just
that.

Spirituality as Academic Discipline

Looking at spirituality as liturgy makes a great deal of sense
to the Church-minded, but an increasing number of authors
wish to free spirituality from the limits of ecclesial domination.
Such a perspective looks at spirituality as an academic discipline,
similar to other behavioral sciences. It is to be studied free from
religious absolutes and seen as an expression of personal transcendence. As such, religious experience, free from God, is an
appropriate field of study in the university.

It is precisely this problem that the American Academy of
Religion confronted in its four-year seminar from 1984 to 1988.
The result of that seminar was published in 1990 in the AAR
series "Studies in Religion" (no. 62), titled *Modern Christian Spirituality*. The study of interpreting a text is called hermeneutics,
and the problems of interpretation that accompany the scientific,
academic study of spirituality are treated in part 1 of the work

(pp. 1–61). The prestigious contributors[6] attempt to address this question: "Does the study of spirituality deserve the status of an academic discipline?" While many universities include courses on great spiritual writers, they are normally examined under various disciplines: philosophy, medieval studies, religious studies, literature, to name a few. But the question being raised in this work is whether or not spirituality ought to be its own discipline.

SPIRITUALITY WITHOUT RELIGION

Sandra Schneiders affirms the legitimacy of spirituality as an academic discipline, but she draws a distinction between "experience" (20–24) and the "discipline" (24–37). This distinction equals the difference between "an experiential trans-cultic reality" and the academic discipline that studies such realities. Preferring the term "spirituality" over "spiritual theology," Schneiders hopes to free it from a historical subservience to "dogmatic and/or moral theology" (27). Spirituality that is "unfreighted" from theology and taken as religious experience requires an interdisciplinary study wherein theology is but one relevant discipline among others (e.g., psychology, comparative religion, anthropology, history, etc.). Consequently, she limits her description of spirituality as "the field of study which attempts to investigate in an interdisciplinary way spiritual experience as such, i.e. as spiritual and as experience" (31). I say limited because the spiritual experience is divorced from its defining religious structures. Earlier Schneiders stated that the subject of this "contemporary discipline" is "the experience of consciously striving to integrate one's life in terms of self-transcendence toward the ultimate value one perceives" (31). This statement is somewhat unsatisfying if it means absolutizing the ego independent of the uncomfortable

---

[6] Sandra Schneiders (Jesuit School of Theology); Ewert Cousins (Fordham University); Bradley Hanson (Luther College); and Carlos Eire (University of Virginia).

reality and inconvenience of "otherness." If one's sense of spirituality is defined by one's own self-actualization, by one's own sense of self-transcendence as perceived by the ego, then it seems no longer significant for one to deal with those other entities that challenge or oppose the ego.

Schneiders gives several characteristics of this new discipline (32–33). First, it is an interdisciplinary discipline. Second, it is a descriptive-critical discipline and not a proscriptive-normative one. Third, it is ecumenical, interreligious, and cross-cultural. And fourth, it is a holistic discipline. Given these characteristics Schneiders observes that spirituality, so defined, bears a striking affinity with feminism (33). This raises some question as to her intention. Is spirituality a discipline in its own right or not? Unfortunately this question remains unanswered. As a practical discipline we are told that spirituality involves a particular type of object, methodological style, and both an objective (or objectifying) as well as an ideal procedure. Simply stated, the individual is the object; it is a participatory method, with pluralistic objectiveness and an appropriating procedure (33–37).

While there is great value in assigning autonomous academic status to spirituality, there is also a real danger. Spirituality comes to be understood without need of a God, just as New Religiosity has been described as religion without God.[7] We may ask, Is the "experience" of God (or what Schneiders calls "self-transcendence toward the ultimate value one perceives") able to be studied through pan-cultural, interdisciplinary, holistic, descriptive lenses without the fundamental binding (*religare*) of the ego to the absolute non-ego (God)? In attempting to make spirituality an emerging discipline freed from theology, Schneiders has spirituality accept other shackles, those of self-preoccupation and a limited notion of truth. If I might put my difficulty with this in a slightly different way: Is it possible to study the experience of a friend in such a disciplined fashion

---

[7] Hubertus Mynarek, *Religiös ohne Gott? Neue Relgiosität der Gegenwart in Selbstzeugnissen* (Berlin: 1983).

without the concrete particularity of this friend's otherness? If one is able to do so, it seems a horrible reduction of the notion of friend, or in this case a lifeless reduction of spirituality.

TRADITION-SPECIFIC SPIRITUALITY

Ewert Cousins in his brief essay recounts the editorial problems he faced with his 1985 publishing project *World Spirituality*.[8] Given the planned inclusion of non-Christian traditions, spirituality had to be defined in terms of the human person's "spiritual core" (40). Therefore, each tradition's editor formulated an appropriate definition for "spirituality."[9] The fact is that these definitions set limits according to the traditions. Such tradition-specificity, according to Cousins, reiterated spirituality's concern with several areas: the experiential, the inner, the real, the transcendent, and the divine (43). However, how does this differ from the contextualization of spirituality by religion itself that Schneiders rejected? Doesn't the term "spirituality" as used by Cousins merely replicate the religious tradition itself? In this case it is fair to hold spirituality as being dependent upon the contextualization of a particular religious and theological tradition. But, we might ask how Schneiders' interest in nonreligious or religion-free spirituality is any different than Cousins. It seems almost impossible to honestly address spirituality without also addressing a religion of some sort.

Cousins points out that McGinn, in the volumes on Christian spirituality, omits any formulation of the essence of Christian spirituality. McGinn believes that the Christian essence will emerge in retrospect with Don Saliers' final volume. A further indication of this confused method was the decision made by

---

[8] Ewert Cousins, ed., *World Spirituality: An Encyclopedic History of the Religious Quest in 25 volumes* (New York: Crossroad Publishing Co., 1985).

[9] Bernard McGinn edited the Christian tradition, Arthur Green was responsible for Judaism, Seyyed Hassein Nasr for Islam, and Krishna Sivaraman had Hinduism.

the Christian editors not to use a chronological ordering. Instead they devoted half of the first volume to doctrinal themes (e.g., Christ, Trinity, *imago dei*, grace) and to praxis (liturgy, prayer, spiritual direction). According to Cousins this indicates that Christian spirituality "proceeds through an experience of Christ, the Trinity, and grace [doctrine], within the life of the community of the Church [praxis]" (43).

What is significant is that this denies, at least for these editors, the possibility of Schneiders' religion-free spirituality. Spirituality needs religion, and Cousins' acknowledgment of this religious specificity is significant if we are to define spirituality. A genuine study of spirituality must preserve the specific aspects of its religious context. This should not be overlooked since it in fact preserves the unique differences in spirituality. Masao Abe[10] had similarly pleaded that in the Buddhist-Christian dialogue each religion's specific aspects contributed more than their similarities.

SPIRITUAL THEOLOGY

Bradley Hanson's chapter opposes Schneiders' notion of an independent discipline and defines it as "spiritual theology or something analogous to it" (45). According to Hanson, if anything is to be considered a field of study, one needs to distinguish in it a distinct subject matter and a distinct approach to that subject matter. Hanson sets up four possible subject matters. They are (1) the self-transcending human spirit, (2) the spiritual core and ultimate reality of a person, (3) self-transcending ultimacy without the ultimate, and (4) lived reality. He then proceeds to reject the distinctiveness of each (46–49). Even though he fails to name a distinct subject matter, he does settle on a distinct approach, which he calls the "investigator's relation to the subject matter" (49). This approach combines "serious reflec-

---

[10] See his *Zen and Western Thought* (Honolulu: University of Hawaii Press, 1985).

tion and strongly existential orientation" (50). According to Hanson spirituality is "that study whose subject matter is faith and which involves a stance of the subject toward the subject matter that combines hard reflection with a strong existential concern to grow in faith" (50). Consequently Hanson concludes that spirituality may not be taken as an academic discipline but is in fact a unique approach to a subject matter that properly belongs to theology. It represents "a stance that ought to infuse much that is done in biblical studies, systematic theology and ethics" (50). Sadly, one might miss the point behind his flurry of academic jargon, so I want to be clear. In the end he is saying that spirituality is about life and faith.

THE VAGUENESS OF SPIRITUALITY

Similarly Carlos Eire's contribution notes the sociological problems in defining spirituality as a discipline in the academy. He reckons that its vagueness is too crippling for such recognition. Emphasis on experience, or Schneiders' field-encompassing field, poses problems requiring several points. First, the concept of reality implied in such experiences needs to be clarified. Second, an analytical method would need to be applied to the structure of spiritual experience. And third, these experiences would need to be related to their social reality (58–59). Eire concludes that in the strict sense it is unlikely that spirituality can be taken as an academic discipline. Rather, "established academic disciplines and the study of spirituality will best coexist and promote each other's well being when their investigations share a common sense of order and direction" (61). Again, simply put, spirituality is too expansive to be reduced to a single discipline of the academy. We see that there is a danger in subjecting spirituality to the canons of a scientific discipline. Both Hanson and Eire support the study of spirituality as dependent upon other established academic disciplines. This suggests that spirituality is either too vague or too pervasive for the academy to address its novelty. In the end, even the academy acknowledges that any fair treatment of spirituality has to maintain this vital link to religion.

Spirituality as History

Perhaps the pervasive character of spirituality demands a context too large for academic scrutiny. After all, a Dominic or an Ignatius stands out, but they do not exhaust the spiritualities that have been assigned to them. Clearly spirituality oozes and warrants a kind of definition that keeps pace with its oozing. Philip Sheldrake's 1995 revision of his earlier *Spirituality & History* offers an understanding of spirituality defined by "historical contextuality." Of the approaches examined thus far Sheldrake's seems to me the most promising. He subjects our understanding of spirituality to the acid bath of rigorous historical study. His aim is much needed in an age that has forgotten the vast sea of human experience beyond the present moment. His alarm is well taken since so much of spirituality demands that capacity of mind to study the texts and times of personalities living centuries away. "This book," he says, "also concentrates on exposing the discipline of spirituality to the contemporary concern with historical skills and interpretation. . . . In particular, it seeks to alert readers and students to the importance of understanding spiritualities in their full historical settings, to the complex issues raised by seeking to organize the details of history into an intelligible pattern, to the need to grasp differences in interpretations of history, and the need to use our sources in a more sophisticated way" (10). Truly Sheldrake's efforts are grander than a history of spirituality. He, in fact, is shifting our focus from the egoist readings to a larger periphery.

HISTORICAL TOOLS

In chapter 1 Sheldrake forces us to rethink history and its use in the study of spirituality. Essentially he brings current historical theory and methods as tools to expose the object of spirituality. By demanding that history strip not only the past but the limits of our own interpretive biases, he forces spirituality to the naked reality of human experience and "the conscious human response to God that is both personal and ecclesial" (45). Chapter 2 sets out in search of a definition for spirituality. In so doing we see that its history instructs us in the complexities of that definition. However, in offering a definition of spirituality Sheldrake is able to say that "this relationship [with God] is lived out, not in isolation, but in a community of believers that is brought into being by commitment to Christ and sustained by the active presence of the Spirit of God in each and in the community as a whole" (61). This leads the way for chapter 3's treatment of the process of history and chapter 4's examination of how we use our spiritual history. Both chapters are instructive in exposing the *locus theologicus* of spirituality in the complexity of human relationships.

Part 2 (113–67) puts forth two case studies (religious life and medieval women's movements) to demonstrate the impact of historical analysis and interpretation. And finally part 3 (169–225) presses the problems in our current uses of spiritual texts (chap. 7) and the hermeneutical questions raised in our typologic discussion of spiritual traditions. In other words, how we read and understand writings from the past. Sheldrake's work is exceptional in forcing the definition of spirituality to embrace the realities of human life, or as he puts it, "not about some other *kind* of life but about *the whole of human life at depth*" (60).

One ought to ask why Sheldrake's approach is so satisfying. In doing so we find that he has placed us at the very embers of a life of faith. The honesty of such a definition contributes to a far more accurate reading of these individuals and why the whole of their lives have spiritual weightiness. Sheldrake's approach forces us to look at spirituality, not outside of this person's situation, but from one's personal immersion in a snag of facts, the givens that time and place hurl at us. And yet, why does a person reckon all this whirl in such a way that names the theophany "Thou," or nobly rises above its tempest to act, even to die contradicting its own apparent logic? Here is where I believe we must move to yet another understanding of spirituality.

Spirituality and Theology

In looking at spirituality the various perspectives not only name a reality but place one in relationship to the object studied. If we choose to look at Christian spirituality, we need to bring to it a way of looking. This demands academic integrity in our views, a sense of reverence and awe for the objects viewed, as well as an appreciation of the historical context or setting. Since Vatican II, theology has broadened its discipline in a way that is at home with the liturgical, academic, and historical interests already mentioned. While some authors would like to lure spirituality into the pseudo-autonomy of an independent academic discipline, such an approach seems terribly lifeless. Any study of Christian spirituality needs to admit its need for a theological perspective. Such an admission means the interdependence of doctrinal concepts and spiritual experience. Their organic integration is an essential part of the *Corpus Christi* motif found in Roman Catholicism (and the Augustinian Christian West as well). It is this one-yet-distinct character of the Church as Body of Christ that requires Christian spirituality to remain intimately linked with Catholic theological discourse. Fundamentally it is the same unity that underlies the unity of the human person, holding spirituality bound to the Christian life. This unity of soul and body is why Catholic thinking rejects the Oriental and New Age notions of reincarnation. Catholic thought holds to the uniqueness of each human existence, that confusingly complex mix of a person's particular time and place so eloquently treated in *Gaudium et Spes*.

While attempts to define spirituality show themselves reaching out to various aspects of the person (liturgy, interdisciplinary studies, or historical context), it seems that the defining core must be found to reside in the person himself or herself. Yet, we see the inadequacies of reducing spirituality to some "thing," isolating spirituality to some "other world" presence in the person. Our predicament is to situate the defining core of spirituality in some personal *res* that is at the same time the very nonpersonal principle of integration for the person. An understanding of spirituality must be able to tie together the manifold aspects of human existence, this unique given of time and place. But, in addition it must be able to integrate the wide range of reality, material reality and whatever more there might be to reality, traditionally called metaphysical reality.

Such a principle of integration has been understood as "the human soul." Apart from some disdain for the concept, it has been preserved in our conceptual lexicon. The doctrine of the soul, on the other hand, has had its own struggles throughout time. The debates might seem esoteric; however, I propose that such debates have in fact not been over metaphysical refinements but rather over the very principle of human integration that we are now seeking. Spirituality has traditionally been seen as the soul's journey to God. Simply put, spirituality is the lifelong integration of a person toward God. What more appropriate term for our defining spirituality than the very principle of its integration. We shall see how the concept of the soul properly defines the spiritual life, and that this definition of spirituality offers us a larger look at Christian spirituality.

Chapter Two

Keeping the Spiritual Life Alive

Problems in defining spirituality arise from the difficulties in how we look at it. Is the ego the proper term for defining spirituality? If so, our definition will be determined by our experiences, our self-transcendence. Or, if we say that God is the proper term, spirituality will be defined in terms of the Absolute. Similarly, if spirituality's defining term is cult, it will emphasize religious culture in its definition. I argue that the proper term for defining spirituality must be the concept of the soul. However, our present understanding of this soul-concept is sadly distorted. Notice how Catherine of Siena (1347–80) is able to speak of the soul with such ease:

> A soul rises up, restless with tremendous desire for God's honor and the salvation of souls. She has for some time exercised herself in virtue and has become accustomed to dwelling in the cell of self-knowledge in order to know better God's goodness toward her, since upon knowledge follows love. And loving, she seeks to pursue truth and clothe herself in it.[1]

[1] Catherine of Siena, *The Dialogue*, trans. Suzanne Noffke (New York: Paulist Press, 1980) 25.

Or how John of the Cross two centuries later (1542–91) grasps its reality:

> This dark night is an inflow of God into the soul that purges it of its habitual ignorance and imperfections, natural and spiritual, and which contemplatives call infused or mystical theology. Through this contemplation, God teaches the soul secretly and instructs it in the perfection of love without its doing anything or understanding how this happens.[2]

Both these writers see the soul as part of a person's fuller understanding of life in relation to God. Under the heading of spirituality, we seek to address something akin to this divine aspect in human personality. Whatever we call this life principle (*nephesh*, *pneuma*, *spiritus*), it will necessarily embrace the difficult existential reality of de facto living. What does my life mean?

All genuine spirituality manifests an ethical living that is seen in a person's lifestyle; she is "clothed in it," as Catherine says, or he is "purged of what it is not," according to John. But how can we speak about souls today, given our sophisticated development of human, scientific, and critical understanding? Even with the many advances of science and technology there remains a haunting vocabulary that is the theological lexicon of the soul. While its grammar is often reduced to the aesthetic rhetoric of late eighteenth- and early nineteenth-century Romanticism (Novalis, Hugo, Blake, Shelley, Byron), it possesses an amazing technical meaning that ought not to be discarded. Our current study of spirituality will be helped if we can retrieve the underlying referent of this soul language as our defining term for spirituality.

Some may recall this common bedtime rhyme: "Now I lay me down to sleep, I pray Thee Lord my soul to keep. If I should die before I wake, I pray Thee Lord my soul to take." This simple

---

[2] *John of the Cross: Selected Writings*, ed. Kieran Kavanaugh, O.C.D. (New York: Paulist Press, 1987) 200–201.

prayer suggests the problem that obscures our fuller understanding of the spiritual life, namely, the nature of the human
soul. Is the soul a separate thing, like my hand or my eye? Or,
is it rather the unifying non-thing of the whole human person?
How we answer this question has a tremendous impact on how
we end up defining spirituality. I argue that the soul-concept is
the proper term for defining spirituality. It is in the life of the
soul, in its intellectual and volitional life, how we think and what
we desire, that one comes to see the proper end of spirituality.

The Life of the Soul

Various authors have employed the soul-concept, most notably
Thomas Moore's *Care of the Soul* and the homey Chicken Soup
for the Soul series. But they miss a fundamental step; they do
not ascertain a truly theological understanding of the soul. If the
soul is taken in the sense of a distinct thing in the person, spiritual life is seen as preserving and safeguarding this essential
core from all the dangerous non-soul "things." However, if we
take the second meaning of soul as integration, we need to acknowledge the radical implications such a pervasive reality has
for studying the human person. "God teaches the soul secretly,"
as John of the Cross rightly observed.

One immediate consequence is that our relation to our world
cannot be restricted to our physical body. To say that the human
soul *qua* soul is one with our body alters our dualistic thinking
about the spiritual life.[3] Consequently here and now, in this
existence, there cannot be an antagonism between the soul and
the body, since the human soul is the integrating principle
(*principium*) of the body. Dualistic notions, which have plagued
a sound understanding of the soul for centuries and even turn

---

[3] See the work done by Caroline Walker Bynum on understandings of
the body in *Fragmentation and Redemption: Essays on Gender and the Human
Body in Medieval Religion* (New York: Zone Books, 1992), and *The Resurrection
of the Body in Western Christianity, 200–1336* (New York: Columbia University
Press, 1995).

up in Moore's work, divide the person, so that body and soul are seen as opposed to each other. The soul is seen as the body's hostage, demanding a ransom for its freedom. In the end, one needs to conquer the body so as to be freed from this "beast of the flesh." If we adopt a grammar that reduces bodily existence to a beast or to something to be fought against, then all materiality, such as the world, which is an extension of human embodiment, and creation itself, are understood in the same conflictual categories. However, this is inconsistent with a theology of divine Incarnation. The soul, and here bear in mind the theological battles fought to safeguard the human aspect of Christ's soul, is the principle of integration, not alienation.

It may be apparent that what I have been calling the integrating soul is in fact St. Thomas Aquinas's rendition of the Aristotelian soul (see Aquinas's *Summa Theologiae* I, q. 75–102). I want to emphasize our need to guard against a contemporary elimination of this metaphysical understanding by its being trivialized. Such a tendency to reduce the human soul to a materially objectify-able (or personified) thing robs humanity of its depth. Rather, the human soul must be preserved as the active principle that unites and integrates the whole of a person's life—that is to say, one's spatial, temporal, historical, material as well as any other additional nonmaterial (or nonphysical) realities of authentic human existence (love, hope, faith). The soul does not simply unite the body, but the soul integrates all of one's bodily, social, and historical relatedness. It integrates a person's past, present, and future. It is the unifying principle of one's moment in a particular human context, as well as the human contexts of the past and the human destiny that unfolds in time and place. It is an active reality holding together the uniqueness of the person. Thomas's sense of the soul is worth lifelong study, but we can only touch upon it here.

The soul is not-a-thing, literally "nothing," and for the great mystics this fact is wherein the soul is most like God. In a soul-centered understanding, spirituality cannot be thought of dualistically, that is, over against the "non-soul." Rather, it must be understood integrally, as the uniting principle of the total person.

This *totus* (the whole person) is not just of the individual person's body but it includes a person's historicity as well. As *principium* the individual human soul not only holds together the particular bodily materiality of the person but it also holds together what we might call the "extended materiality of the non-ego." Let me explain. We wrongly think about ourselves in individualistic and autonomous ways, isolated from our world and from others. Yes, who I am is unique, but I am more. I am woven into manifold dimensions beyond my subjectivity. We are always immersed in a sea of realities that we integrate into the meaning of our life. People, places, and things have an integral pull at who we are, and the soul integrates these realities, and this animates us. Who I am is a galaxy of relationships to people and places, to moments in my life and hopes that are yet to be born.

It is this last element that offers us a safeguard against the moral-volitional indifference of Quietism (Miguel de Molinos) and the devotional anti-intellectualism of Pietism (August Hermann Francke) by requiring us to look not only at the isolated individual person but also at the person's entire commerce of practical and theoretical activities. What are the things that move a person beyond the self (what moves someone to action, what moves someone to know, what moves someone to love)? Perhaps if we substitute the term "motivation," we come closer to the technical sense of *motio*. The soul moves us! Consequently, our thinking about "spirituality" needs to take into account the full scope of this vast motivating arena. The kind of integration intended here is of the people (friends and foes), places (home and hinterland), times (thens, nows and not-nows), and the technology (telecommunication media) that extend human activity. The concept of soul that I am proposing is not only the metaphysically integrating principle of one's particular existence but it is also the motivating life principle of personal human existence. Simply put, the soul not only is the unique holding together (*principium*) of one's historicity, it is also that which moves one to full "actualization" (potentiality to actuality). This is very important, for truly caring for the soul is all about one's destiny.

We may take this life of the soul to be the source of a person's unique living in two ways. First, it is through the soul's capacity to move a person toward understanding, toward knowing one's self and other "non-self" realities that one comes to the true self. This is accomplished through human intelligence, or through speculation regarding theories about reality. (I shall set aside the problem surrounding the absolute or universal claims made on behalf of these theories for other works.) In the second way, the soul-concept possesses the power to move one toward specific goals or desirable objects for no other reason than for the apparent good these objects suggest. Perhaps a more acceptable phrasing of this would be to say that what "moves" or motivates each of us is a twofold desire: (1) a desire for the things that are good; and (2) a desire to understand these good things (in themselves) that we desire, or the why of our desiring the things we desire. Consequently, the soul exerts its principle of integration and motivates one to live both the moral-volitional life of desires as well as the intellectual life of meaning. With such a model for understanding spiritual life, that is, one that takes the soul not as an object but as the pervasive principle, we establish for ourselves a corrective for evaluating spirituality in both its "traditional" forms and in its less apparent forms. In the study of spirituality, or the spiritual life, we must pay attention to the intellectual life and the moral-volitional life, or as Catherine put it, "upon knowledge follows love."

The Intellectually Meaningful Life

The "intellectual life" of the soul incorporates all manners and modes of expressing and articulating one's spiritual life. It is possible for us to reduce our understanding of "intellectual" to mean just one's capacity for abstraction and speculation. We forget that it also has to include what is called the "right brain," our nonverbal creativity. Western culture has been profoundly marked by the logos of Greek philosophy. One cannot deny that this is the West's bedrock reality inherited from the traditions of Plato and Aristotle. Western Christianity, being inescapably marked by Western culture, always needs to address its Platonic and Aristotelian ancestry. However, Western Christianity has also acquired several formative corrective elements that serve to significantly recast Greek intellectual life.

First, the Christian Logos is qualified by the *debar Elohim* of the Jewish wisdom tradition with both its sense of divine prophetic revelation and of divine efficacious creativity. The word of God, the *debar Elohim*, goes forth and does not return empty but has its impact. It is not only the prophetic word of God but the acting word of God as well. Not only is it the word with which God speaks to the people of God but it is the word of God at work in the people of God. It is to this latter reality that we have access, the word spoken and not the word speaking. Second, the Greek logos has been reformed by the revelation of Jesus Christ and the Church's Trinitarian doctrine, with its mysterious notion of oneness in the Godhead yet there mysteriously being a distinction of persons. In other words, because of its Trinitarian notion of God, Christianity has handed on a Logos that is identified with the second person of the Triune God, existing in relationship so that there is essentially distinction in person of the Word but also a natural unity in relation to the Trinity itself. Third, the Reformation and Counter-Reformation, with Protestantism's stress upon the inspired (written) Word of Scriptures, was also formative. The struggle between *sola scriptura* and *traditio et scriptura* marks this period's Humanist shaping of the Greek logos along with an emphasis on the knowing subject. And finally, the impact of the Second Vatican Council with its agenda for renewal and ecumenism in the face of increasing secularization has shaped our appropriation of the Logos now in the notion of *Dignitatis Humanae*, which I believe upon closer reading is a modern transposition of the medieval soul-concept.

Unfortunately elements of the Enlightenment and many more secondary variables have left religiously minded folk with a faith-understanding that is either intimidated by scientific understanding, or suspicious of it, or at the very least bored with academic inquiry. Our intellectually meaningful self is more receptive than we think and is not satisfied for long with the superficial understandings we try to force on it. While today a person has "access" to greater information, it does not necessarily mean that he or she has greater knowledge. Our "knowing" can become, on the one hand, so superficial that we are afraid to engage the deeper issues necessary to confront differing points of view; or on the other hand, our knowledge can become so specialized that we are unable to even visit other truths due to our ideological blind spots. "Spiritual life" (taken as the life of the soul) breaks down these obstacles and integrates one's life experience in a fashion satisfying to human understanding. Spirituality or the spiritual life of the soul needs to understand, but in a way that satisfies the lived reality.

The spiritual traditions we study are lived traditions embodied in specific viable lifestyles; they are not abstract ideas. Rather than limiting the "intellectual life" to the cerebral realm, it is necessary for us to expand our thinking and admit with classical theology that the "intellectual life" is a life that is immersed in the human project of naming wisdom. What has slowly and steadily been forgotten in the increasingly secularized Christian West is that its Logos does not remain in the "mind" but goes forth bringing about its purpose (Incarnation/redemption). If we work to preserve this wisdom naming activity of the intellectual life, we will more clearly see the necessary link to the moral-volitional life of the soul. Intellectual life does not indicate a vague unliving thing simply limited to abstract ideas. While abstract ideas (or *theoria*) are important in our avoiding superficiality, at the same time one needs to avoid any overspecialization that limits or mutes the manifold languages of wisdom. The classical notion of philosophy is as "a love of wisdom," and in that sense the intellectual life is the naming of that wisdom in the community, in the world, in religious faith. This wisdom dimension of the spiritual life needs to be recognized in the spiritual lifestyles of the "spiritualities" we study. Now let us look at the volitional life of the soul.

The Morally Desirable Life

In examining the moral or volitional life of the soul, it must be kept in mind that the soul is the integrating principle. This means that it is not divided into a thinking soul and a desiring soul; rather, the soul is one. However, traditionally the powers or capacities that the soul manifests are twofold—to know and to love. The volitional life of the soul, or its power to move the person toward the good object, calls one into varying worlds of commerce. Because the will compels the individual to move toward some desirable object, it pushes the person out into a world of competing desires. Examples of this would be the appetite for food, the appetite for pleasure, the desire for well-being. In all of these desires, and more, the will moves the individual to want these good objects. At the same time it is moving and placing a person into various worlds other than its own. In this the soul forces the individual to move out from self, into other realities—hunting down one's prey, gathering food, comforting one's self with shelter, pursuing sexual satisfaction, contending with sickness, and grieving over death or loss. Were this movement determined by desire alone, or merely the volitional "willing" without the ethical, then the important link to the intellectual life would be severed. Spiritual life would be reduced to the desires of the ego's Nietzschean "will to power." But we know that the spiritual life must have an ethical dimension. The soul seeks to integrate humanity in both of its powers—knowing and desiring. Spirituality is not about the object as good in itself but what and how we come to know that this good is a good; this is what gives life to the soul. Spirituality isn't about praying because praying is a good thing but it is, as John of the Cross says, "God teach[ing] the soul secretly and instruct[ing] it in the perfection of love." The ethical life is, in fact, that practical life that is the soul's integration. It satisfies both in light of its desires as well as its hunger to understand. Our desires, because they imply ethical actions, force us to reflect upon these desires. Whatever good objects I'm drawn to, at some point because of the ethical concern, I come to ask the question, what is this thing's worth?

There is a necessary relatedness between the intellectual and the moral. However, it is in the face of an unguided or undisciplined will (i.e., one severed from the intellect) that a hermeneutics of suspicion alienates the human, seeking justification for desire rather than reasonably directing such desires. Modernity has made us aware that economic forces, psychological motives, and philosophical concepts are at play within the spiritual life. Consequently we have discovered that when the will has no moral limit and simply seeks to addictively consume, no true integration occurs. The Modern compulsion to consumerism and materialism more than suggests that something is disoriented in human life. Our suspicions lead us to question economic, psychological, and philosophical motives at work (to examine our conscience). While the will desires what it perceives to be the good object, it is human reason that must name rightly the desires. For example, something seems to be good, and I am seductively drawn to it, but it is the intellect that names the goodness in it and why it is sought or its badness and why it is repulsed. Hunger brings me to stand gazing into the refrigerator as though it were the eighth wonder of the world, but it is my intellect that in this case judges the salad to be a greater good than the chocolate cake. Similarly, while it is human reason that articulates this perception, it is only the will, the moral-volitional life, that acts on its desire. In other words, there is a complementary relation between these two faculties of the soul. The soul integrates inasmuch as the volition compels one to desire some good thing and moves the individual toward that good thing. However, it is only the intellect that names that good as truly good. The other side of this is that the intellect cannot act; it motivates. Only the will acts upon desire (*orexis*); the intellect is "along for the ride."

Caution needs to be taken so as not to presume that either the intellectual or moral-ethical provides clarity or precision or decisive actions. The far greater experience of the spiritual life is the prophetic and infallible sense (a sense of "rightness" of action that is inexplicable) that this manner of living is right and in agreement with God's revelation in Christ and in the "mystery" of Church. Examples of this abound in people like Catherine of Siena, Francis of Assisi, or Rose of Lima. Another danger common to students of spirituality is to focus on the text alone and presume that the text is the person. One must bear in mind that you, as reader, always bring yourself to the text. How can one retain the historicity of the text and the individual's integrity? If we only look at the text, we reduce it to a philological reading and reduce spiritual life to some pristine intellectual realm. We ought not to forget that the *debar Elohim* of Israel, the word of God that goes forth and does not return empty, is an active word, and as such it is not only the written script but it is the word as the living tradition as well. Only when we recognize the vitality of spirituality will we claim its fullest meaning.

Soul-centered: *Psyche* or *Anima*?

In much of the literature on spirituality one can see an ever-increasing dependency on the behavioral sciences (psychology and sociology) to interpret and define religious (spiritual) experience. While Christian spirituality needs the behavioral sciences as a valuable tool, especially given the soul's pervasive and integrative character, it cannot reduce spiritual life to psychological factors at the expense of all the doctrinal factors, those teachings that guide us in the truth. The spiritual life must enliven, animate the faith. The Latin term for soul is *anima*, but we in the West often use its Greek equivalent, *psyche*. Unfortunately this has reduced the soul and the spiritual life to a mere psychology. It is more correct for us in the Latin West to speak of the soul in terms of its animating capacity. At its best, Christian spirituality may be defined as an existential animation of the Christian doctrine that is both intellectually satisfying and morally desirable. Such a spiritual lifestyle rests in the soul's unifying presence, which uniquely integrates the vast arena of one's human existence. This relational reality takes place in the event of integration, which is at the heart, and soul, of spiritual life.

The individual soul integrates all of one's experiences. It is not something separate from one's body, but permeates it. It is not something that simply permeates the body, but enters into and integrates all relationships with various persons, places, and things. It is precisely this sense of life that animates spirituality. For the Christian recognizes in the doctrine of the Incarnation, God made flesh, that our flesh is one with this Christ. This animates spiritual life and opposes the psychological motives that reduce spiritual life to internal mechanics that rationalize life. Was Catherine of Siena anorexic? Is this the core of her spirituality? Does a reduction to psychological or physiological data explain Catherine? Isn't it more important to say that even so, all the dimensions of Catherine's life and what they ultimately came to mean for her arose from the integrating principle of her soul? Theology cannot abandon spirituality to a discipline of the academy since spirituality animates the doctrines theology has struggled to name. This is important because in a certain sense doctrines can be seen as a concentrated distillation of the spiritual life. The images and metaphors that the spiritual writer uses and the lifestyle he or she encourages serve to animate the doctrines of faith. Spirituality, as the integration of the givens of life with meaning and desire, reveals the spiritual woman or man as a kind of neuron of an age, integrating the whirl of life. Now the questions that are asked move us beyond a core of beliefs. Instead they dislocate and relocate the intellect and the will in a process of animated integration, making life meaningful and desirable.

Animation?

Animation as used in the film industry is a process that brings the text (graphics) to life. I believe that a theological notion of animation similarly brings the text (doctrine) to life. The interplay between a person's perception of one graphic and the next, their relative location to one graphic and the next, the time and sequence of each graphic, the details and relations of these details all make for a successful animation. One can honestly say it is the "soul" of the Disney animated feature. Similarly a theological animation involves the perception a person has of one graphic (read as doctrine) and the next, the relative location of doctrines and their order and duration in the movement. Imagine any great spiritual writers—Hildegard of Bingen, Bernard of Clairvaux, Thomas Merton—and picture the way in which doctrines of their faith played an intimate role in their spirituality. Of these doctrines, note what details and how the relation of these details will animate them, setting the reality in right relation. There must be an integration of all these factors so that doctrines are animated. For example, Catherine of Siena can only be under- stood in light of her life, its *complexus* of time and place, of loca- tion and dislocation, which for her relied on the doctrine of the Incarnation. This doctrinal graphic is animated in the "bridging" of her life, which is in Christ who is the bridge of her life:

> Then God eternal, to stir up even more that soul's love for the salvation of souls, responded to her: Before I show you what I want to show you, and what you asked to see, I want to describe the bridge for you. I have told you that it stretches from heaven to earth by reason of my having joined myself with your humanity, which I formed from the earth's clay. This bridge, my only-begotten Son, has three stairs. Two of them he built on the wood of the most holy cross, and the third even as he tasted the great bitterness of the gall and vinegar they gave him to drink. You will recognize in these three stairs three spiritual stages.[4]

In this graphic the reality of Catherine's fragmented life finds its integration in the doctrine of the Incarnation of Christ. This *anima*tion bridges Catholic doctrine and life. *Anima*tion, as a theological concept, deals with a person's location and disloca-

---

[4] Noffke, *The Dialogue*, 64.

tion, a sense of human integration, and meaningfulness. By retrieving a theological understanding of the soul, I see two important benefits.

Important Benefits

First, the theological concept of soul holds a profoundly humanizing corrective for our reading of spirituality. It sets forth a fuller understanding of the person that is both intellectual and volitional. Any interpretation of spirituality that is not intellectually and morally satisfying fails true human flourishing. It is necessarily suspect due to its disintegration of the human community and of the human person. This means that spirituality read through the corrective of the soul can be seen as the integration of the personal and social dimensions of each person. To the degree that a person's life is an example of such integration, he or she testifies to a genuine spiritual integration. This witness animates, beyond a particular moment, and generates in others the capacity for integration, promoting truly human existence. Spirituality sails on the winds of particular human endeavors and attempts to integrate the vast sea of human existence, passing from person to person and from age to age. This explains why we might find solace in one spiritual lifestyle and not in another, why we move from one to another at different times in our lives, and why two similar people might find integration in two completely different spiritual lifestyles. However, the crucial reality must remain the intellectual and volitional drive of human existence. Consequently, a spiritual lifestyle that lacks intellectual and moral integrity is not properly speaking spirituality. This is crucial on the practical and pastoral level as one must deal with the myriad of destructive pseudo-spiritualities. Theologically this means that the intellectual and moral integration of a Christian spirituality must address the clumsy bundle of an incarnation that is both personal (in Christ) and social (Christ's Body, the Church).

The second benefit is the necessary location and dislocation of the ego that the soul requires. The soul as a principle of integration is both ego and non-ego, which allows self to confront non-self. It is a Magnificat of ultimate meaning not unlike Mary's prayer: "My soul proclaims the greatness of the Lord" (Luke 1:46).[5] The concept of the soul demands a critique of human subjectivity as well as a critique of the very horizon of human existence, the ground of being. Mary knew this only too well! Recall how she asked, "How can this be?" To save one's soul means a dislocation of the ego beyond subjectivity.[6] Again, Mary's letting go in her response: "let it happen to me as you have said" (Luke 1:38). It transcends the specificity of human limitation and forces the ego to redefine itself in terms of the non-ego. An example of this can be seen in human intimacy and the passion of such love/lust. The ego, drawn by the intensity of its desires, faces the violence of its own limitations and either violates the object of desire or confronts a redefining of itself not by the other, but by the intercourse of self and non-self. One wrestles with demons and with angels in this dislocation. Ecstasy is quite literally the dislocation of ego, the being-out-of-place (*ek-stasis*). Ecstasy is something more than orgasm; it is the loss of self, the letting go of control, which dislocates the ego. This intercourse of self and non-self defies discourse, and yet it is an ineffable reality beyond subjectivity. Similarly the concept of soul confronts human limitation and dislocates ego beyond subjectivity. The concept of soul, with its radical dislocation, pushes our reading of spirituality to look for integration. This intellectual and moral integration, which moves beyond subjectivity

---

[5] All Scripture quotations are from the New Jerusalem Bible (1985).

[6] On the topic of otherness the works of Emmanuel Levinas are extremely instructive, especially: *Existence and Existents*, trans. Alphonso Lingis (Hague: Nijhoff, 1978); *Ethics and Infinity*, trans. Richard A. Cohen (Pittsburgh: Duquesne University Press, 1985); *Time and the Other and Additional Essays*, trans. Richard A. Cohen (Pittsburgh: Duquesne University Press, 1987); and *Outside the Subject*, trans. Michael B. Smith (Stanford: Stanford University Press, 1994).

and dislocates the ego, is the animating role of spiritual life. Animation gives life to doctrine and a true spirituality animates true doctrine. The dislocated ego is forced to the ecstatic scream that cries out not "I" but "Thou"!

Chapter Three

Animating Spirituality

Christianity's magisterial teaching on the soul is its under-standing of human flourishing. When the soul is taken as the principle of integration we see that several variables are at play: (1) me, (2) my relation to the world, and (3) the beliefs that shape who I am. For the sake of argument I will call these self, life, and doctrine. This is all well and good as a tool for study, but the reality is that these three factors don't neatly line up. They are dynamic and changing so, in the end, all we can do is be mindful of their presence as we study spirituality and allow them to guide our reading. If you want to study something that is dynamic, you need to do so actively. This helps us to animate the spiritualities we study. Spirituality is about much more than the self. True spirituality achieves integration. It brings to life and animates the self, human life, and religious doctrine. But, in addition, the self desires knowledge and love, and in this, every spiritual writing is about knowing and loving. Nothing more captures the human soul than these two hungers, to know and to love our ultimate end. It is why God made us! However, this takes place in very specific realities that we generally call life. And, in that tautological reality of living life, each one of us wrestles with the basic questions of "Where am I?" and "What or who am I?" This is our default menu and we see it every time we meet someone new. After our exchange of names, in a second level of reflection, our point of reference as human beings is to ask about our origin ("From where do I come?") and our destiny, our direction or purpose ("Where am I going?"). We see this as the standard, for most polite conversation centers on this. Introductions are about where you come from and what you do. The depth of our answers to each of these indicate various levels of familiarity and trust as we disclose more about our true self. So much can be discovered in asking these basic questions (perhaps painfully so, strapped into your seat on a nine-hour flight).

In studying spirituality we attempt to explore the manner of integration found at work in an individual, the mix of one's self, one's life, and one's beliefs. The self or "I" that is attempting to bring together the knowing and loving does so in order to constitute a sense of self. But the study of spirituality has another task and that is to examine the life of this person as well—to try to understand the lived reality of the person whose life manifests this spirituality. The proper object of spirituality is the ethical and intellectual integrity of this manner of life. But, I believe that the study of spirituality has a further task—to explore the beliefs behind this spirituality. What dimension of belief enables a person to surmount life's challenges? This level of critical engagement is most important for getting at the animating sense of spirituality. Doctrines take shape because of a human need to focus life's meaning. They serve as a kind of collective shorthand for a variety of lived experiences and the distillation of these experiences. Whether they are revealed by God or arise from human genius, they capture an important part of the human project that is realized by the community. How these doctrines both shape a specific spirituality, and at the same time are critiqued by this spirituality, is an essential part of our study. Two such doctrines that hold particular religious significance will normally address the community's sense of where "we" came from and where "we" are going. The competing doctrines of creationism based on revelation and evolutionism based on science are examples of the formative power doctrines hold. So how can we study spirituality and retain its animating dimension?

Methodology: What Does Spirituality Examine?

In an attempt to systematically study the great spiritual writers we need to establish a method. One will readily note that every method has its own limits and what I propose is not meant to be exhaustive. It is, you will see, a valuable tool, a kind of checklist to make sure that one adequately examines each spirituality and spiritual tradition. As I have already said, self, life, and doctrine provide the three key factors necessary for a critical evaluation of spirituality. While I am focusing on the Christian tradition, a similar case can be made for any of the "varieties of religious experience" (William James). Whether it is Catherine of Siena or Madame Helena Blavatsky, we need to examine the person, the life context, and the doctrinal factors at work in forming a particular spirituality. Each of these factors will require our addressing two important concepts, which each in turn imply a continuum of thought for our writers. Maintaining a mutual correlation of these factors helps to ensure a fuller reading of the spiritual writing and a more complete understanding of the particular spirituality being studied. Take Catherine of Siena, for example. It is a poor reading of her spirituality if we cherry-pick quotes we like. We need to study her life and her struggles, but at the same time we need to observe how she understood the world in which she lived and us as creatures. One might stop there and only read Catherine as a self-actualized individual. To do so would be a mistake because it amputates her theological project that is written into her spiritual life. To fairly study spirituality and a writer like Catherine, we must also look at the community's body of belief that guides, forms, and transforms a person. I think this is the something more we long for, the something more missing from our lives, the something more that changes who we are.

For the sake of easy reference the table below sketches what I am addressing. In studying spirituality the (1) self, (2) life, and (3) doctrine are excavated in looking at the concepts at work in a spirituality. I use this verb deliberately because it requires work, our "digging up" ideas. Any spirituality's capacity to integrate can be critically evaluated by examining the continuum for these concepts. For example, the concepts of integration and transcendence help us appreciate the individual's sense of self. When we ask the critical questions about their integration as being one of relationship or isolation, we critically assess this concept in a particular spirituality. In addition to the table, a look at how it works will make better sense of this approach.

Factors	Concepts	Continuum
Self	Integration	Isolation-Relation
	Transcendence	Location-Dislocation
Life	Cosmology	Chaos-Order
	Anthropology	Autonomy-Solidarity
Doctrine	Creation	Human-Divine
	Redemption	Damnation-Salvation

How the Factors Work

We can get a better sense of these factors if we look at a passage from one of the greatest spiritual writers of the early Church, Gregory of Nyssa. The following excerpt demonstrates how these essential factors of self, life, and doctrine dynamically shape the spiritual life. In this work Gregory is addressing the Christian life:

> If anyone withdraws his attention for a moment from his body and, emerging from the slavery of his passions and his carelessness, looks at his own soul with honest and sincere reason,

he will see clearly how its nature reveals God's love for us and His intention in creating us. Reflecting in this manner, he will discover as essential and natural to man an impulse of his will towards the beautiful and the best, and connected with his nature a passionless and blessed love of that intelligible and blessed image of which man is the imitation. However, a certain illusion related to the visible and the changing, caused by unreasonable emotion and bitter pleasure, always deceives and beguiles the soul which is careless and unguarded because of indifference, and drags it to terrible evil, originating in the pleasures of life, begetting death for those who love it. It is for this reason that the knowledge of the truth, the saving medicine for our soul is, by the grace of our Saviour, bestowed as a gift upon those who accept it eagerly. By this grace, the illusion beguiling man is dispelled, the dishonoring preoccupation with the flesh is extinguished and by the light of truth, the soul which received the knowledge, makes its way to the divine, and to its own salvation.[1]

Many of us might have lost interest reading even a brief text like this, and we overlook what the text is offering. However, if we want to learn from a text its spirituality, we need to find ways to engage it, and that is what these three factors allow. They provide us with valuable tools to highlight and to engage the text, and the person of the text, in a more complete way. Let me demonstrate what I mean by using these three factors to engage Gregory in a more complete way.

SELF: QUESTIONS OF INTEGRATION AND TRANSCENDENCE

In looking at the person, the sense of self, we attempt to discover the person behind the spirituality. To do so there are two concepts we need to address: (1) the person's sense of integration and (2) his or her sense of transcendence. In other words, how

---

[1] Gregory of Nyssa, "On the Christian Mode of Life," in *Ascetical Works*, trans. Virginia Woods Callahan, The Fathers of the Church Series, vol. 58 (Washington, DC: Catholic University of America Press, 1967) 127.

a person holds it all together and is able to rise above the limits. To the first concept of integration one might ask, *How does he or she piece the world together?* and, *Where does he or she fit in the big picture?* To do this we explore the continuum of thought at work in his or her writings. This continuum that we explore is the writer's sense of isolation on the one hand and sense of relation on the other. Our study of a spiritual writer needs to ask about his or her "fit." Does the person see oneself as alone, besieged, abandoned, persecuted, enslaved, a stranger in his or her own home? This is an important assessment to make in reading the spiritual writer. Does the writer call for movement from such isolation toward a sense of relation? For example, how are we to understand Gregory of Nyssa when he wrote, "However, a certain illusion related to the visible and the changing, caused by unreasonable emotion and bitter pleasure, always deceives and beguiles the soul which is careless and unguarded because of indifference, and drags it to terrible evil, originating in the pleasures of life, begetting death for those who love it" ("Christian Mode of Life," 127)? This sense of isolation requires us to ask how Gregory attempts to achieve integration, movement toward a greater sense of relation.

Gregory demonstrates a second concept that we need to address, the concept of transcendence. This is the notion of the self's rising above its limitations. The continuum that this suggests is that of a sense of location, the "where am I" of a person, and a sense of dislocation, a being "out of place." No longer does one locate the self in a particular situation, but in this sense of dislocation, our "out-of-place-ness," the spiritual writer reshapes the world. These examples of transcendence, of dislocation, in the spiritual writer are ones that we ought not to ignore. In studying spirituality we see the self longing, desiring some hyper-reality that comes to make sense in this question of transcendence. It plays an instrumental role in the sense of self, the "who" that speaks. We see this when Gregory writes, "It is for this reason that the knowledge of the truth, the saving medicine for our soul is, by the grace of our Saviour, bestowed as a gift upon those who accept it eagerly" (ibid.).

LIFE: QUESTIONS OF COSMOLOGY AND ANTHROPOLOGY

The second factor one needs to systematically explore, if we want to critically appreciate spirituality, is that of life or the person's context. Spirituality, as animating, draws into itself the worlds of varying concerns and commerce. All of this comes to be seen as we explore the concepts of cosmology and anthropology. Cosmology, one's view of the world, introduces the continuum of chaos and order into our study. Here is where the historical, sociological, and psychological tools are especially helpful as we attempt to understand their world. The traditional historical approach to spirituality is not adequate if we take history in a dialectical sense. Rather, the behavioral sciences all provide important tools for catching a glimpse of the life-world at play in this spirituality. As I will demonstrate, spirituality is a world of meaning that shapes the individual around key beliefs. So even though a historical approach opens the door, this "life factor" requires our examining the roles and responsibilities given to the spiritual writer and the way in which humanity was understood during his or her lifetime. This brings up the concept of anthropology. Whereas cosmology puts before us the dimension of chaos and order in a person's life, anthropology holds up the continuum of autonomy and solidarity—how the person understands self in relation to other realities.

Take another look at Gregory of Nyssa. We cannot appreciate his spirituality without a sense of the world in which he lived and his own sense of that world. To neglect his life reduces his spirituality to a greeting card, a nice, cute saying for me and my friends. Gregory's spirituality has to be read in light of the fourth century's political chaos created by the Nicene and Arian debates. The Arian influences on the emperor Valens and Gregory's strong ties with his older brother Basil and another Nicene sympathizer named Gregory are part of his spirituality. The association and support of these three men from Cappadocia and their roles as bishops of Nyssa, Caesarea, and Nazianzus are significant factors in Gregory's spirituality. Gregory's association with these men, his banishment that ends with Valens's death, and the sympathetic support of Emperor Theodosius and the western emperor Valentinian are integral aspects of Gregory's spirituality. The movement from chaos to order, from autonomy to solidarity, helps to animate this spirituality and our sense of its worth. It enriches our reading of the spirituality and its role in the human project.

Again, if we now look at the two sentences just above where we started evaluating Gregory, we begin to see how this animating look at spirituality assists our reading the spiritual writers. Gregory states, "If anyone withdraws his attention for a moment from his body and, emerging from the slavery of his passions and his carelessness, looks at his own soul with honest and sincere reason, he will see clearly how its nature reveals God's love for us and His intention in creating us. Reflecting in this manner, he will discover as essential and natural to man an impulse of his will towards the beautiful and the best, and connected with his nature a passionless and blessed love of that intelligible and blessed image of which man is the imitation" ("Christian Mode of Life," 127). The sense of order found in Gregory's world and his sense of solidarity with the heart of that world are clearly found in this opening to his work "On the Christian Mode of Life." There is in human nature a sense of solidarity that draws one to the order of the cosmos as beautiful, perfect, and intelligible. But why? Why does Gregory, given his historical realities, come to this sense of his life and his world? What causes any spiritual writer to integrate the fragmentary realities of his or her world and hold them together in a new way? The answer is found in exploring our third factor, that of doctrine.

DOCTRINE: QUESTIONS OF CREATION AND REDEMPTION

In asking about doctrine, our study of spirituality brings to the fore two concepts that help us to understand the spiritual writer; they are creation and redemption. How does a writer understand the story of creation? Here a complete study of spirituality has to explore the continuum of the human and divine, creature and Creator. The way one's religious tradition defines creation—its sense of the human, or the divine, or both, at work in creation—is crucial in the way a spiritual writer will integrate his or her life. Along with a sense of our origin found in creation, the doctrinal teaching on redemption, our ultimate destiny, also shapes our reading of spirituality. In the doctrine of redemption (or its equivalent) a community names its sense of salvation and damnation—how they fulfill their role in humanity or their failure to do so. This last continuum raises questions as to a spirituality's sense of salvation. There is an ultimate destiny! If we only focus on the reading and do not ask the question of doctrinal integration, we are left with a partial reading of Gregory. Again, we can turn to Gregory of Nyssa as a helpful illustration. One needs to ask the question as to why Gregory is able to integrate the disparate bits of his life in a way that is intellectually satisfying and morally desirable. His doctrinal integration emerges in the next sentence: "It is for this reason that the knowledge of the truth, the saving medicine for our soul is, by the grace of our Saviour, bestowed as a gift upon those who accept it eagerly. By this grace, the illusion beguiling man is dispelled, the dishonoring preoccupation with the flesh is extinguished and by the light of truth, the soul which received the knowledge, makes its way to the divine, and to its own salvation" ("Christian Mode of Life," 127). This third level of reflection on spirituality takes seriously the doctrinal aspect of religious mindedness. One comes to an animating sense of Gregory's spirituality in his sense of the Nicene faith and its preservation of the divinity of Jesus Christ. Only a humanity so embraced by God can set right Gregory's life context and Gregory's place in it all. If created human nature were not receptive to this kind of redemption, seen in the reality of Jesus Christ, then Gregory's life itself would not be open to rising above the trials and tribulations. For Gregory, the Nicene doctrine of the Incarnation enabled him to say that one "will see clearly how its nature [human nature] reveals God's love for us and His intention in creating us" (ibid.). Human nature, because of Christ's Incarnation, is the doctrine animated in the reality of Gregory and his spirituality.

Approaching Spirituality

As we can see, a fuller study of spirituality takes place if we are able to keep these three factors of self, life, and doctrine in mind. Begin with the self, and the life world of the self. But, I believe something more arises in the way doctrines bring a person to look at his or her reality, not from the perspective of the ego alone, or just the historical facts of the age. This is where we see the animating perspective of religious faith. If we try to keep these factors as dynamic guides, we see how the concepts and their continua set in motion the complexus that is involved in an animated reading of spirituality. For some, diagrams can be helpful to visualize what this approach entails. The following diagram suggests the concerns that weave in and through the complex reality of a spiritual life. Let's look first at the self. The self encounters its world and presents its concerns as to life in the world. This implies eight aspects related to the four concepts: integration, transcendence, cosmology, anthropology. The self must face integration—how one feels in relation to or isolated from one's world. The questions of transcendence address a sense of personal location or dislocation. By reflecting upon the sense of self in a spirituality, how the spiritual writer conveys both relationality and location, we are put in touch with a dimension of the text that is both personal to the author and at the same time universal to humanity. This is what makes spirituality a place where theology is animated.

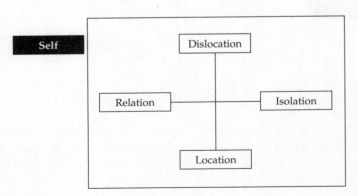

Next, by placing on top of the self, with its questions of integration and transcendence, the added factor of life with its questions of cosmology and anthropology, we now open the text to the world of the author, a world that puts his or her spirituality in a lived context. By exploring how a particular spirituality puts forth a worldview that is ordered and full of meaning, we see how a spirituality offers a sense of one's humanity that is fulfilled in solidarity. We are able to see the various life contexts that can be paradigmatic for numerous people with similar life contexts. Pastorally this is of value in recommending one spirituality to a person and not another. How we see our world and humanity are connected to how we live life. Morality is first and foremost an existential, lived reality. Chaos, for example, leads a person to isolation of the self and dislocation, a failure to belong. Order, on the other hand, contributes to a sense of location and relation. What is of note is how autonomy gives one a sense of location apart from, isolated from, the other (lower right triangular portion of diagram). It is solidarity that allows one to be dislocated yet related, both to self and non-self (upper left triangular portion of diagram).

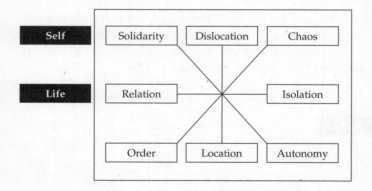

All great spiritualities embody teaching, doctrines that guide one in the face of one's living life. They teach their disciples about creation itself and one's ultimate destiny. Theologically these concepts can be spoken of as creation and redemption. Is our world something of our own design or is it something more? Damnation would wrongly have us believe that the self can choose to ultimately be about chaos, isolation, and dislocation (upper right triangular portion of diagram), while salvation teaches one to seek order, relation, and location (lower left triangular portion of diagram).

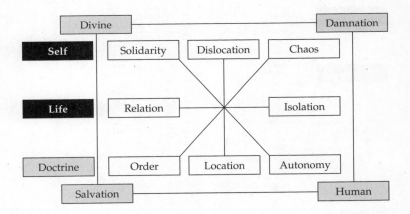

Doctrine possesses an additional capacity. It is also able to flip one's sense of self and one's sense of life. It can provide a paradoxically inverted way of looking at one's self and one's life. The divine is the inversion of the human, and salvation inverts damnation. Doctrine affords one the capacity to see realities from the other side, so to say.

The study of spirituality must attend to these realities. But notice, and this will seem strange at first, it is with doctrine that the self and life are reoriented, flipped, twisted, and turned. See page 48. This is what I mean by theological animation of doctrine and life. There is another way to look at the mountains. Gregory was able to look at his reality and choose to live contrary to the will of the powers that be because of his belief in the true humanity of Christ, a doctrine of belief that put everything else into perspective. Secular Humanists may be inspiring, but they are not spiritual. On one level we could stop our reading of spirituality with just the two factors of self and life, a two-dimensional Polaroid. While adequate, it would be incomplete, lacking the added dimension of doctrine. So what does this mean to our method of reading spirituality?

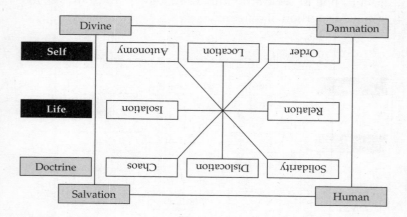

Summary

Spirituality is theology. It is a practical, lived theology, a theology not written in words but in lives. My approach to spirituality is one that stresses this animating quality. Christian spirituality brings life to doctrines and animates them, in the person and in his or her life context, discovering a new level of meaning. Consequently, each genuine spirituality contains a theological animation that resonates with other people in other times who share a similar mix of self, life, and doctrine. As theology, spirituality must not only be viewed from the text but the context as well, the larger realities that shape the text.

I do not believe that a traditional history of spirituality does justice to the reality of spirituality. What follows will be a look at spirituality that keeps these three factors in view. While a historical approach is a customary framing, I don't believe that spirituality reduces to its historical components. Although the historical periods are helpful and have become standard historical divisions,[2] I see spirituality as animating life and doctrine in four general ways: (1) *ascetical*, which aims at integrating a more or less biblical cosmology amid the human struggles that were part of the early Church; (2) *mystical-metaphysical*, which arose out of the cultural context of medieval European university and city life with a noetic cosmology and speculative inquiry into the mind of God; (3) *aesthetical*, which confronted a fracturing of sacred structures within the social climate of Humanist subjectivity and the Galilean-Newtonian cosmologies; and, (4) *social-critical*, which emerges with the industrial and technological revolutions. It is today marked by the awkward uncertainty of the New Physics and the short-lived po-mo (Post-Modern) chaos. What is important is the particular integration of factors. Therefore, I treat spirituality as exemplary of individuals who integrate a particular life world, and who, in their integration, reflect the fuller understanding of the human project. Finally this animating approach to spirituality provides a limit to the definition of spirituality in light of its doctrinal dimension. While poetry or art or literature can be inspirational, they are only properly considered spiritual in their ability to animate genuine doctrine. In studying Christian spirituality as Christians, we can only speak of non-Christian or secular writers as spiritual to the extent that they animate the doctrinal understanding of the Christian community. Consequently doctrinal integration provides a standard for identifying what is Christian spirituality and what is not. One could use this approach to study other spiritual traditions mindful of its formative and doctrinal elements. So by extension, what

---

[2] Pierre Pourrat's 1927 study of Christian spirituality is arranged in four volumes: (1) "From the Time of our Lord till the Dawn of the Middle Ages," (2) "In the Middles Ages," (3) "Later Developments: From the Renaissance to Jansenism," and (4) "Later Developments: From Jansenism to Modern Times." It has a significant impact in the historical study of spirituality and was translated into the English by Newman Press in Maryland (1953–55).

is Jewish spirituality and what is not, or Buddhist, Muslim, etc., and what is not.

Yes, indeed, something has been missing for so many of us, something more that we know is there, something more that makes our lives meaningful, something more that makes living desirable. There is something more to be found in this living of our lives. We can begin to discover this something more in learning from the lives of women and men who were spiritually animated, whose lives were meaningful and satisfying.

Part II

Spiritual Animation

Man's intimate relationship with God in the Holy Spirit also enables him to understand himself, his own humanity, in a new way. Thus that image and likeness of God which man is from his very beginning is fully realized. This intimate truth of the human being has to be continually rediscovered in the light of Christ who is the prototype of the relationship with God. There also has to be rediscovered in Christ the reason for "full self-discovery through a sincere gift of himself" to others, as the Second Vatican Council writes: precisely by reason of this divine likeness which "shows that on earth man . . . is the only creature that God wishes for himself" in his dignity as a person, but as one open to integration and social communion. The effective knowledge and full implementation of this truth of his being come about only by the power of the Holy Spirit. Man learns this truth from Jesus Christ and puts it into practice in his own life by the power of the Spirit, whom Jesus himself has given to us.

Along this path—the path of such an inner maturity, which includes the full discovery of the meaning of humanity— God comes close to man, and permeates more and more completely the whole human world. The Triune God, who "exists" in himself as a transcendent reality of interpersonal gift, giving himself in the Holy Spirit as gift to man, transforms the human world from within, from inside hearts and minds. Along this path the world, made to share in the divine gift, becomes—as the Council teaches—"ever more human, ever more profoundly human," while within the world, through people's hearts and minds, the Kingdom develops in which God will be definitively "all in all": as gift and love. Gift and love: this is the eternal power of the opening of the Triune God to the world, in the Holy Spirit.

John Paul II
Dominum et Vivificantem (59)

While this animating approach invites a fuller reading of spirituality, it also affords a unique perspective to our study. The doctrinal questions of creation and redemption in Christianity are two chords that bring us back to our refrain on the life of the soul. Life, with its changing perceptions on humanity and the cosmos, presses the Christian community to doctrinally clarify its understanding of God's revelation in light of lived experience. The realities that give rise to new forms of spirituality are this same encounter with life and divine revelation. Here is where we see spiritual writers as exemplary of ways of living that integrate doctrine and life.

We can appreciate spirituality by studying an individual who embodies and is exemplary of a spiritual integration. We might choose to study Adrienne von Speyr and begin with her reality (her studies, marriage, career, friendships) and consider her life context and the way she integrated her faith and its beliefs into a kind of spirituality. But there is another "back door" approach to the study of spirituality. It is possible for us to begin by studying the dynamics of life and the way doctrines address life realities, giving rise to definable spiritualities. An individual, like Adrienne von Speyr, manifests her spirituality, not as part of the *status quo*, but because of raw new realities in understanding her world, humanity, its destiny, and its role in this new reality.

I propose to look at the traditional types of spirituality (ascetical, mystical, aesthetical, and social-critical) from the perspective of life context and the Christian community's need to magisterially define the Christian meaning of these specific contexts. Both dogmatic theologian and spiritual author are part of an ongoing revelation in the Christian community. In this approach we see that the variables present in life arise in history but are not historically limited. We can wrongly have the sense that asceticism was only for the early Church, or mysticism for the medieval Church. Spirituality is perennial and surfaces again and again in people's lives. This happens because these variables are timeless and present themselves throughout history. My approach here will be to address the life context, by which I mean to draw from the historical setting but not limit myself to a period in history. A context is a blend of various realities manifest in time but it is always expressive of other realities. I focus on the historical articulation of a context's cosmology and anthropology that has either challenged or served to clarify the Christian doctrines. We can see this most clearly when the Church acts to decisively safeguard the community in dogmatic teaching that holds forth the revelation on the true dignity of human existence, the question of the human soul. In doing so we are able to see the common project of theology and spirituality in individual women and men who exemplify an integration of doctrine and life for the Christian community.

Chapter Four

Run the Good Race:
The Ascetical Approach

Meet an Ascetic: Maximus the Confessor

The best way to appreciate spiritual traditions is to meet those women and men who lived them. It is unlikely that we might expect to meet an ascetic walking down the street. So when we think of an ascetical approach to spirituality, we imagine it is long gone. But, as we will see, there are ascetics even today. We might ask why they would choose such a disciplined life, what would motivate them to go without comforts that we deem essential. But once we meet ascetics we realize that their spirituality encounters the realities of their lives. Their circumstances and their ultimate beliefs have fashioned lives that have meaning and that are morally desirable. It's when we look beyond the superficial impression we may have of ascetics that we discover how the factors of self, life, and doctrine foster a way to integrate their lives and animate their beliefs. We can then better appreciate what it was in them that made them look for that something more missing from their lives.

In Maximus the Confessor we find a sophisticated Byzantian, born in Constantinople (ca. 580) and educated for civil service to the empire. At the age of about thirty-four he left public life and entered a monastery, only to flee the invasion of the Persians in 626. At almost fifty, he had already lived in Crete, Cyprus, and Carthage, having written extensively in defense of the two natures in Christ. It was his strong desire to preserve the human nature of Christ against those who advocated eliminating his human will (called Monothelites) that likely led Pope Martin I to invite Maximus to participate in a synod held at Lateran (649). Now, imagine a man almost seventy years of age deciding to oppose this heresy, especially given an imperial ban of 647. Emperor Constans II, in his *Typos*, had prohibited all discussion on the will in Christ. So what would motivate this old man to risk losing everything? Be sure that in his disregarding this ban Maximus, along with Pope Martin, was forced to Constantinople in 655 on charges of treason. There they were tortured and finally exiled to Thrace.

It seems that even this imperial action did not weaken the old Maximus, who continued to force the discussion, maintaining two natures in Christ, specifically preserving the integrity of Christ's human nature and his human will. The price paid by this eighty-two-year-old saintly man for his heroic defense of Christ's humanity was that he had his tongue and right hand cut off. He died not long after, in exile on the Black Sea. The Monothelite question wasn't settled until 681 when the Council of Constantinople defined the two wills in Christ's nature, preserving the freedom of Christ's human will yet stressing the harmony of these two wills.

Why would Maximus risk his comfort and even his life because of what some might consider an insignificant belief? We can discover an answer in Maximus's work *The Ascetic Life*,[1] where he explains the value of asceticism. In it "a brother" asks "the old man" who can imitate Christ. The old man tells him,

---

[1] St. Maximus the Confessor, *The Ascetic Life*, trans. Polycarp Sherwood, O.S.B., Ancient Christian Writers vol. 21 (Westminster, MD: Newman Press, 1955).

"None of those enslaved to material things can imitate the Lord. . . . But those who can say: 'Behold, we have left all and followed Thee,' these receive the power both to imitate Him and to do well in all His commandments" (105). He goes on to have the old man explain the reality of discipleship:

> Therefore, he who wants to be His disciple and to be found worthy of Him, and to receive power from Him against the spirits of wickedness, will separate himself from eery fleshly attachment and strip himself of every worldly passion. And thus he contends with the invisible enemies in behalf of His commandments, just as the Lord Himself set an example for us in being tried both in the desert by their chief and, returned to the civilization, by the demoniacs. (105–6)

The brother laments the challenge of so many commands and his own limitation, to which the old man replies:

> Though they are many, brother, yet they are all summed up in one word: *Thou shalt love the Lord thy God with thy whole strength, and with thy whole mind, and thy neighbor as thyself.* And he who strives to keep this word succeeds with all the commandments together. And no one that does not separate himself as was said before, from passion for worldly things, can love genuinely either God or his neighbor. Indeed, at the same time to attend to the material and to love God, simply cannot be. This is what the Lord says: *No man can serve two masters*; and: *No man can serve God and mammon.* For so far as our mind clings to the things of the world, it is their slave and scornfully transgresses God's commandment. (106)

In the life and writings of Maximus, we meet the ascetic who is striving to integrate dimensions of his spirituality. His life, with its cosmology of struggle and its anthropology united in Christ, animates his doctrinal belief in the human soul's unique creation by God and its ultimate destiny. The human will in Christ makes the struggles of our own human will viable. In the particulars of Maximus's life, we see that his facing persecution and physical punishment only makes sense in his belief of something beyond himself. "No man can serve two masters . . . for so far as our mind clings to the things of the world, it is their slave and scornfully transgresses God's commandment." So what is it that makes an ascetic be an ascetic? Now that we have met one, let's look more closely at the factors that help us critically understand asceticism.

Ascetic Spirituality

The ascetical tradition is a blending of the Greek philosophical and the Hebrew biblical cosmologies as Christianity moved beyond its familiar terrain. This raised new questions about the human person. The Platonic view of the world and the Genesis-Pauline account of the cosmos set a context for animation that confronted the Gnostic and Stoic perspectives. Consequently the formative teaching of Christian doctrine on human nature plays a key role. This is seen in the physical training and mental discipline that is asceticism.

Christianity has been unmistakably influenced by the Greek way of looking at the world. This cultural reality has wiggled its way into Western culture, and it has deposited in the womb of our ideas, ideals about life, the world, and ultimate reality. So central is this Greek vision that many of our Western notions about the state, the person, and God have been transmitted to us in very Greek fashion—*polis* (politics), *anthropos* (anthropology), and *theos* (theology). There is an almost natural affinity between this Greek vision and much of what the West desires. Even with modern *techne* (technology) there is an abiding longing for ancient *sophia* (wisdom). This is why modern men and women are never too far from the cosmos of the ancient Greeks. In part, this is also due to its ability to satisfy our questions, to make meaning of this vast mystery we call our world. Central to this cosmology has been the thought of Plato and Aristotle. I would like to offer a general account of that cosmology that brings divine order to what is otherwise chaos.

We human beings find our location by coming to know the order of things. Because there is order, we come to sense that there is some ordering principle at work. Our knowing moves from an imperfect knowing to a more perfect knowing. This capacity for knowing determines reality. Knowing marks the Hellenic passion that even today makes the world of knowledge (*nous*) or for some, virtual reality, more real than the experiential world that surrounds us. It is in this climate that the reality of soul is first perceived as the principle of motion in a thing. Technically, this is either by growth, called "augmentation," or movement, called "locomotion." Humans move and grow from some inner principle. This led to more developed theories about the life principle called the soul. Here the influence of Plato, on the one hand, and Aristotle, on the other, proposes two distinct visions of reality that impact all subsequent interpretive models. Volumes have been written on the philosophy of these two thinkers, and we do not need to rehearse those labors here. Rather, the concept of "form" demonstrates the distinct cosmologies born of the Hellenic desire to know.

In Plato, especially in his more mature works of the *Phaedo* and the *Republic*, we see that intellectual and moral perfection moves toward the world of form or idea. This perfection occurs not in the world of change but only by an inner turning to the perfection within of knowing itself, that is, the soul (*Phaedo* 79D). Here we see the dialectic between form and matter, unseen and seen, underlying the dualism of soul and body. Consequently, reality, what is most real, is perfect knowing in the soul. This approach was attacked by Plato's own disciple Aristotle, who dismissed it as vacuous (*Anal. post.* 83a 33). Rather, Aristotle emphasizes the actual existence of a thing's becoming "that which it is to be" or *entelechy*. In *De Anima* (412–13) Aristotle sees the soul as just such an actualization of particular material existence itself. He preferred this view over Plato's because human existence is seen as a unified substantial reality. The reality of human existence is in fact this actualization of bodily becoming. Here we can appreciate Aristotle's emphasis on causality as justifying his departure from Plato. Reality is the thing itself, and our universal conceptions are abstracted from our knowledge of these things. This knowledge is of the soul, but taken in two ways, the knowledge and the knowing.

Knowing creates a world of meaning and purpose. For Plato, the creation of things involved primary incorporeal substances called *hypostasis*. One such nonmaterial *hypostasis* is the World Soul, out of which all human souls are composed. Both the World Soul and Nous emanate out from the One. They emanate from the One in levels or ranks. One of these emanations is Intellect (*nous*) and another is the World Soul (*psyche*). Human souls (*hypostases*) are part eternal ("divine"), but because they are composed, they are also part of the material world of becoming. The perfect world exists without becoming, whereas the imperfect world, our world, is becoming. The spiritual world is understood as being part of the perfect world, and we humans enter this spiritual world in our being perfected in contemplation. There is no change in the perfect world, while the material world is imperfect, becoming, changing, untrustworthy. It actualizes different potencies, and in this imperfect world there are always different potentials, different possibilities both good and bad. In the perfect world there are no such possibilities because it is complete, and as such it is foreign to us. The Greeks understood the human soul as part divine (part perfect), but it was materially composed with body, which meant it was becoming, and lacking in perfection. This "composition" suggested a constant tension between the two worlds—that of perfect being and imperfect becoming. Plato explained the cause for this tension in the human person as deriving from a division in the soul itself, which is divided into three parts: the rational soul, the irascible (passionate) soul, and the appetitive (desirous) soul (cf. *Timeaus* 69D–72B; *Phaedo* 80B; *Republic* 4.444B). The conflict between these three competing "souls" in the human person could only achieve harmony by the rational soul's superior control over the other two souls of human passion and desire. This constant inner struggle between the divine perfection and the earthly imperfection is why the human souls were seen as part of the divine

World Soul's ongoing cosmic struggle. The world offered by Aristotle's notion of *entelechy* promised a solution to this tension. He saw that the soul must be inseparable from its body if the thing was to actually exist. In other words, Aristotle understood there to be a necessary union of matter and form so that the soul is the actualization (form) of its potentiality (the body). The uniqueness of this existence is that matter and form are non-dualistically one. For Aristotle form and matter are the intrinsic causes of the thing. He puts it even more simply. The soul is the dynamic (*energia*) that constitutes the human person. We need to look at this again. The soul is a dynamic activity that makes the human person. It is not a thing but a dynamic "making be." It is as though the soul is that perfect pitch to which every instrument of our being resonates. No wonder we can have so many "soul stirring" experiences.

Early Christianity was not only part Greek but it also inherited a Hebrew notion of soul as *nephesh* or life principle in the sense of Genesis 2:7 ("Yahweh God shaped man from the soil of the ground and blew the breath of life into his nostrils, and man became a living being"). As such it was closely tied to life itself and expressed a totality of the person. Occasionally the more Hellenic-minded Paul used *psyche* (soul) and *pneuma* (breath) synonymously and contrasted *psyche* with *soma* (body) and *pneuma* with *sarx* (flesh). Paul, who was a bridge between Jewish and Gentile worlds, demonstrates a preference for *pneuma* over *psyche* because of his emphasis on the role of God's Spirit in salvation. He wants to tie parallels between the *pneuma* of God's spirit in the world and our life principle. Paul takes from the philosophical world and shapes it to his own purpose. The Spirit of God comes through Christ and is opposed to the spirit of this world. The Greek influence upon Paul and his understanding of God, Christ and the Spirit of God lead him toward a triadic understanding of the person as mind (*nous*), flesh (*sarx*), and the conscious subject (*ego*). Paul writes:

We are well aware that the Law is spiritual [*pneuma*]: but I am a creature of flesh and blood [*sarx*] sold as a slave to sin. I do not understand my own behaviour; I do not act as I mean to, but I do things that I hate. While I am acting as I do not want to, I still acknowledge the Law as good, so it is not myself acting, but the sin which lives in me. And really, I know of nothing good living in me—in my natural self, that is—for though the will to do what is good is in me, the power to do it is not: the good thing I want to do, I never do; the evil thing which I do not want—that is what I do. (Rom 7:14-19)

Or in his letter to the Galatians:

Instead, I tell you, be guided by the Spirit, and you will no longer yield to self-indulgence. The desires of self-indulgence [*sarx*] are always in opposition to the Spirit [*pneuma*], and the desires of the Spirit are in opposition to self-indulgence: they are opposites, one against the other; that is how you are prevented from doing the things that you want to. But when you are led by the Spirit, you are not under the Law. When self-indulgence is at work the results are obvious: sexual vice, impurity, and sensuality, the worship of false gods and sorcery; antagonisms and rivalry, jealousy, bad temper and quarrels, disagreements, factions and malice, drunkenness, orgies and all such things. And about these, I tell you now as I have told you in the past, that people who behave in these ways will not inherit the kingdom of God. On the other hand the fruit of the Spirit is love, joy, peace, patience, kindness, goodness, trustfulness, gentleness and self-control; no law can touch such things as these. All who belong to Christ Jesus have crucified self with all its passions and its desires. (Gal 5:16-24)

It is precisely this "spiritual nature" in the human person that makes it possible for the divine Spirit to dwell in each person. Paul wants to avoid the dualistic traps of this soul/*psyche* language used by the Greeks, yet he also wants to recognize the crucial relation between the flesh and the spirit. Paul's anthropology is a cautious one. In Christianity's efforts to understand itself we see how spirituality and theology unfold alongside one another.

Early Christianity

The early Christian writers did not directly treat an understanding of the soul, but rather they indirectly did so by addressing the question of immortality. Athenagoras (ca. 177) held that the immortal soul would be reunited with its body at the resurrection. Irenaeus's (ca. 130–200) work *Against Heresies* (*Adversus haereses*) was an early corrective to the false Platonic cosmology of the demiurge and the errors in understanding they implied. In Irenaeus's comment on the story of Lazarus and the rich man (Luke 16:19-31) he argues in favor of the distinct formal character of a unique "bodily" existence that is recognizable even after the material body of Lazarus "died" (*Adv. haer.* II, 34). This implies an early distinction between materiality and corporeality, between matter and form. A quick overview of some writers will help us to see the early Church's thinking about the soul.

In Clement of Alexandria (ca. 150–215) we see an eclectic employment of Platonism and Stoicism favoring a kind of division in the soul united under one governing power. Clement adopts a trichotomy in the human person of body, soul, and mind (*nous*), but there is not to be found a clear definition of the soul as a spiritual substance. However, we do see this in Clement's pupil, Origen (185–254). In his *De principe*, Origen holds to the singularity of the human soul as a rational substance, that is, a simple rational substance that "grows" in its knowing. Consequently right knowing is essential. We see that what is happening is that a Christian doctrine of the soul is taking shape, and Greek understandings of intellect play a key role. For Christianity the Greek understanding of Logos (*nous*) becomes something parallel with the Judeo-Christian understanding of the Incarnate Word of God. While there are concerns with reducing God to a mere philosophical being, Christianity provides a corrective to this abstract understanding of the Logos in that the Word is made flesh. In this aspect mind, or soul, is the intellectual image of God. Unfortunately, Origen saw the human body as resulting from the soul's being tested by God (Origenism). He argued that just like wax that hardens as it cools, so too the soul that is distant from the warmth of just things finds itself becoming hardened as an embodied soul. In other words our bodily existence is a result of our failure to be close to God. The problem with this can be seen when we reflect on Christ's embodiment. How can that be a failure to be near to God? Finally, Gregory of Nyssa (ca. 330–95) identifies the soul with a rational substance, and this substance is the organic principle of a unique body, endowing the body with the capacity for sensation and self-motion. In his *De hominis opificio* (*The Workings of the Human Being*) the soul is one in nature; it is intellectual and immaterial, possessing powers that it gives to the material body.[2] In Gregory, Christianity begins to form its doctrine of the soul. Here we see that the notion of the soul as the integrating principle, having the powers of intellect and will, is put forth, but the "soul" is not the intellect and it is not will. These are both understood as powers of the soul. The soul gives these two powers for the fulfillment of human existence.

For these Christian writers there is a reciprocity in this union of soul and body—the soul empowers body, enlivening the body; while the body, through its senses, communicates the outer world to the intellect (soul). We now see how a doctrine defines and guides us in a right understanding. In the Latin West, Tertullian (ca. 160–ca. 225), while consistently Christian on the union of body and soul, introduced the error of Traducianism. This held that it was propagation that "procreated" the human soul and not God's unique creative act. This Christianity rejected. It is later, with the great Doctor of the Church Augustine (354–430), that we find a somewhat precise understanding of the soul. Augustine's anthropology begins with the total person being created by God. Body and soul compose the person in a natural union and not as a punitive union. Clearly our soul's being in the body is not punishment. It is important for us to give Augustine a proper reading, and to recognize that history's interpretation of him, salted by Platonic thought, has done him a disservice in

---

[2] J.P. Migne, *Patrologia Graeca* (Paris, 1857–66) 44:176B.

many ways. This is not to say that Augustine is not, in a sense, Platonic, but he is a Christian Platonist. For him the soul remains the active principle and the body the passive, receiving life and form from the soul. Augustine acknowledges the uniqueness of each soul created by God, not seeing it as emanating from some impersonal world soul. This uniqueness of the soul, created by God alone, is a key Christian doctrine. However, we must acknowledge that Augustine remains a bit vague as to the soul's exact origin.

We can see from this brief survey that early Christians encountered the world of their day. They faced an understanding of the soul, human nature, and they were shaped by the light of their faith. For the Church, this was not just a philosophical argument. We see that such questions were at the heart of understanding Jesus and what his Incarnation meant for humanity. It was their communal coming to name the doctrine of the soul that allowed them to appreciate the reality of the Incarnation. Our existence finds its meaning in the incarnate existence of Christ.

My Struggle Is One with Christ

As we look at this formative context, it is important for our study of spirituality to ask what was set in motion by the cosmological and anthropological meanings at play. Thinkers, like those just examined, fostered within the Church particular magisterial instruction regarding the soul (that is, the human person). In turning our attention to the Church's doctrine on the soul, we enter a very different factor in this *anima*tion. No longer are we in that free arena of philosophical speculation, but now we engage the pastoral tradition of the Church as teacher, spiritual guide, and shepherd of souls. One must bear in mind that doctrinal faith is of a different genre than philosophical speculation. The task of any philosopher is to bring her or his understanding to the light of day, while the magisterial task is always intended to be instructive, communal, and consonant. This is important to note. It is *instructive* for the uncertainty of its day, *communal* for the building up of the Body of Christ, the Church, and *consonant* for its consistency with the revelation of God in Christ and in human history. It is, in the long run, a merciful fact that such pronouncements have been limited. When we look to such "teaching" on the soul we discover that these magisterial interventions have been modest, yet extremely formative, of the Catholic doctrine on the soul. This doctrinal guide also forms us and helps us to rightly understand our full humanity amid the uncertainties of life.

Irenaeus (ca. 130–200) gives us a sense of the dangers and the perceived need for magisterial "instruction" on the nature of human existence. He says, "Inasmuch as certain men have set the truth aside, and bring in lying words and vain genealogies, which, as the apostle says 'minister questions rather than godly edifying which is in faith' and by means of their craftily-constructed plausibilities draw away the minds of the inexperienced and take them captive" (*Adv. haer.* I,1). The religious community's need to instruct makes the question of heresy critical in examining the spiritual life, and Irenaeus offers a catalogue of what he considers to be these Gnostic errors. He indicates the dangers of such an appealing system that fools even earnest people.

> Error, indeed, is never set forth in its naked deformity, lest, being thus exposed, it should at once be detected. But it is craftily decked out in an attractive dress, so as, by its outward form, to make it appear to the inexperienced (ridiculous as the expression may seem) more true than the truth itself. One far superior to me has well said, in reference to this point, "A clever imitation in glass casts contempt, as it were, on the precious jewel the emerald (which is most highly esteemed by some), unless it come under the eye of one able to test and expose the counterfeit. Or, again, what inexperienced person can with ease detect the presence of brass when it has been mixed up with silver?" (*Adv. haer.* I,2)

So given the many Gnostic and Stoic understandings of the cosmos and human existence, the Church was pastorally required to give magisterial instruction.

RESPONSE TO GNOSTICISM

Perhaps no cosmology and anthropology rivaled Christianity more than that of the Gnostics, especially in its fourth-century sect known as Manichaeism, which stretched from Persia to as far west as Rome and as far east as China. It preached a dualistic cosmology of two kingdoms in opposition, Light and Darkness, or Good and Evil, which served to explain the origin of the material world, of evil and sin. The Manichaeans distorted aspects of St. Paul and Christianity, holding to a series of three creations: (1) the Kingdom of Darkness created Adam and Eve as a countermove to trap the Kingdom of Light; (2) this Light or Knowledge was set free by the "passible Jesus," who is not only cast into all things but also personifies all the Light that has been mixed into matter; (3) in the end the final Hunter of Light or sometimes Fisher of Light, called "Great Thought," comes to catch the dissipated Light. According to one Gnostic text:

> At the end, when the cosmos is dissolved, this same Thought of Life shall gather himself in and shall form his Soul in the shape of the Last Statue. His net is his Living Spirit, for with his Spirit he shall catch the Light and the Life that is in all things and build it onto his own body.[3]

Such rival notions of the cosmos that in the end corrupted Christian life required a formative stance on the part of the Catholic faith.

As early as 543, the provincial council of Constantinople dealt with a misunderstanding of Origen held by certain Palestinian monks (Origenists). Some called Isochrists held that in the ultimate sharing in the grace of salvation all angels, human persons, and devils would become equal to Christ (called *Apocatastasis* or Universalism) and that all the human souls preexisted but had turned cold in their love of God. For this reason they were

---

[3] Hans Jonas, *The Gnostic Religion* (Boston: Beacon Press, 1958) 235.

cast into bodies as punishment. These positions are so opposed to the uniqueness of the soul and its unique destiny.

Both of these positions were anathematized at that 543 local council, and eighteen years later in Braga, Spain (561) a similar local council of bishops met and condemned the Manichaean and Priscillian doctrine of the soul as composed of the same substance as God (Denzinger 235/*The Church Teaches* 325).[4] The Braga Council specifically rejected the idea of embodiment as punishment (Denz. 236/TCT 326), as well as the notion that human souls were linked to fateful stars (Denz. 239/TCT 329). There is a Christian understanding of the soul as uniquely created by God and individually accountable.

However, it was not until 870 and the Fourth Council of Constantinople that a positive definition of the soul was given to the Western Church. Pope Hadrian II (867–72) and the council took the occasion to declare:

> The Old and the New Testament both teach that humans have one rational, intellectual soul. All the Fathers and the teachers of the Church emphatically affirm this same opinion in their theological discourses. Nevertheless, there are some, zealous in the pursuit of evil, who have come to such a state of godlessness that they boldly teach that humans have two souls. And with a wisdom that has turned to foolishness, these people make irrational attempts to confirm their heresy. And so this holy universal council, makes haste to uproot this evil cockle that is germinating an evil doctrine. Indeed, with the winnowing fan of truth in hand, and with the desire to cast all chaff into the unquenchable fire and to show forth the clean threshing floor of Christ, this council loudly declares anathema both those who originate and those who propagate this godlessness and all those who hold similar opinions. It defines

[4] References to Denzinger (*Enchiridion symbolorum*), 29th edition, are from *The Church Teaches: Documents of the Church in English Translation,* trans. J. Clarkson, J. Edwards, W. Kelly, and J. Welch (St. Louis: B. Herder Book Co., 1955), reprinted by permission of Saint Benedict Press, DBA TAN Books. Hereafter noted as Denz. followed by its number with the English citation following, e.g., Denz. 235/TCT 325.

and promulgates that no one at all may have or keep in any way the doctrine of these authors of godlessness. If anyone presumes to go contrary to this great and holy council: let that one be anathema and be separated from the faith and the worship of Christians. (Denz. 338/TCT 333)

In studying spirituality the cosmological and anthropological factors we discussed in part 1 serve to disclose a world caught in struggle between good and evil, light and darkness. The fundamental question of human existence could be seen as one of isolation on the one hand, literally an alien in this material world doomed to struggle, or on the other hand, related to Christ, and in solidarity with Christ, the struggle is met and the foe is vanquished.

Christian Asceticism: The Victor's Crown

My purpose in this section has been to demonstrate that spiritual life of a specific believer seeks to animate doctrine and life by relating them in a specific time and place so as to witness to some sense of the divine (God) present to the very soul (person) of this believer living in this time and place. Here is where we bring our critical understanding to spirituality and discover its fuller meaning. By engaging the factors of cosmology and anthropology, we enlarge the scope of our reading of a spiritual tradition. Take care, though, that the purpose of animation is not that these factors *ipso facto* constitute a spiritual lifestyle. In studying a specific spiritual writer we must keep in view that this person, at this time, brings together in his or her life a doctrinal reality that integrates and thereby animates true doctrine. In other words, it is the doctrine of Christ's humanity in the redemptive suffering of the Incarnation that is made alive, animated in the ascetical tradition. It is in a context of struggle, one of light and darkness, spirit and flesh, good and evil, that Christ's humanity finds special meaning.

Most often we understand the ascetical life as gray and wracked with pain. Basil the Great (ca. 330–79) in his "Discourse on Ascetical Discipline" does little to change that view. "The monk should own nothing in this world, but he should have as his possessions solitude of the body, modesty of bearing, a modulated tone of voice, and a well-ordered manner of speech." The work proceeds in similar fashion: "He [the monk] ought to think much but speak little, be not forward in speech nor given to useless discoursing, not easily moved to laughter, respectful in bearing, keeping his eyes cast down and his spirit uplifted . . ."[5] Our question might be, how on earth could this approach animate a spiritual lifestyle?

Interestingly we discover that this ascetical way of integration seems to take on athletic and combative characteristics. What animates this approach in the ascetic is a clear and certain sense that the soul has a goal to which it strives and must train, be disciplined, in order to achieve it. John Cassian (ca. 360–after 430) was a great Egyptian monk and spiritual model for centuries. He begins his *Conferences* with Abbot Moses asking two disciples named Cassian and Germanus, "tell me then what is the end and the objective which inspires you to endure all these trials so gladly?" (*Conferences* I,2, p. 38).[6] Their answer, "the Kingdom of God," is accepted by the wise abbot but he pushes them, asking, "But now what should be our aim, what direction should we take which, if closely followed will bring us to our objective?" (ibid., 39). The ascetical training, we see, has a specific purpose that gives meaning here and now. Abbot Moses forces Cassian and Germanus to recognize that the objective is purity of heart now, which is about human flourishing. Cassian observes, "In other words, it is as though he [Abbot Moses] said that you have purity of heart for an objective and eternal life as the goal." Linking this new perspective of Abbot Moses with the magiste-

---

[5] St. Basil, *Ascetical Works*, trans. Monica Wagner, The Fathers of the Church Series, vol. 9 (Washington, DC: Catholic University of America Press, 1962) 33.

[6] John Cassian, *Conferences*, trans. Colm Luibheid (New York: Paulist Press, 1985).

rial words of Paul (Phil 3:13-14), Cassian continues, seeing the running of the good race in a new way. He says, "It is as if the apostle said 'Guided by this aim of forgetting my past, namely the sins of the earlier man, I am driving myself toward the goal of a heavenly reward'" (ibid., 40). But the abbot stresses that the objective is purity of heart. Note that this is an anthropological reality that integrates through virtuous activity and transcends by love:

> Everything we do, our every objective, must be undertaken for the sake of this purity of heart. This is why we take on loneliness, fasting, vigils, work, nakedness. For this we must practice the reading of the Scriptures, together with all the other virtuous activities, and we do so to trap and to hold our hearts free of the harm of every dangerous passion and in order to rise step by step to the high point of love. (ibid., 41)

Even St. Basil (ca. 330–79) had a sense of this challenge and warned against a person undertaking "the cross-bearing life of the monks." After praising the choice a person may make to live in lowliness, he warns:

> But, I beseech you, let no man do this thoughtlessly, nor promise himself an easy existence and salvation without a struggle. He should, rather, undergo rigorous preliminary discipline with a view to proving his fitness to endure tribulations both of body and soul. Lest, exposing himself to unforeseen stratagems, he be unable to resist the assaults against him and find himself in full retreat to his starting point, a victim of disgrace and ridicule. (*Ascetical Works*, Fathers, vol. 9, p. 15)

Some ascetical writers offer a more domesticated variety of striving even in the midst of acknowledging one's own imperfections. Interestingly Basil's younger brother, Gregory of Nyssa (ca. 330–ca. 395), in his *On Perfection* presents another ascetical approach. He begins by commending those who requested his instruction and their desire to grow in perfection. However, he regrets not being able to point to these things in his own life, furnishing as he says "the instruction you seek through deeds rather than word." Notice how Gregory ties his Christology to the Christian vocation. "Our good Master, Jesus Christ, bestowed on us a partnership in His revered name, so that we get our name from no other person connected with us" (*Ascetical Works*, *Fathers*, vol. 58, p. 95). The ascetical practice of conforming ourselves to the name we bear is presented by Gregory not in the discipline of the athlete but in that of the artist. Here we see how Gregory animates the striving of the spiritual ascetic with his magisterial doctrine of conformity to Christ in the discipline of an artist:

> Just as when we are learning the art of painting, the teacher puts before us on a panel a beautifully executed model, and it is necessary for each student to imitate in every way the beauty of that model on his own panel, so that the panels of all will be adorned in accordance with the example of the beauty set before them. (ibid., 110)

There is a doctrinal guide to the image we project of the soul in its conforming to the model of Christ. What follows is pure genius on the part of Gregory in bringing together the self with the factors of life and doctrine:

> In the same way, since every person is the painter of his own life, and choice is the craftsman of the work, and the virtues are the paints for executing the image, there is no small danger that the imitation may change the Prototype into a hateful and ugly person instead of reproducing the master form if we sketch in the character of evil with muddy colors. But, since it is possible, one must prepare the pure colors of the virtues, mixing them with each other according to some artistic formula for the imitation of beauty, so that we become an image of the image, having achieved the beauty of the Prototype through activity as a kind of imitation, as did Paul, who became an "imitator of Christ," through his life of virtue. (ibid., 110–11)

What is clearly seen is the spiritual animation of our conformity to Christ that is made possible through living a virtuous life amid life's struggle, so that the person will achieve for himself or herself "the beauty of the Prototype through activity as a kind of imitation."

The reputations of those ascetics who truly animated doctrine and life got around. John Cassian recounts a fact-finding trip he took to Egypt, where he visited "the greatest possible number of holy men in the remotest areas of the desert of Thebais." Emphasizing their fame, he goes on: "Their renown had spread throughout the world and our urge was not so much to rival them as to get to know them" (*Conferences* XI, p. 141). One almost gets the sense of one football team "scouting out" another rival team's plays and strategies. Even Augustine (d. 430), who searched far and wide for answers to his life's meaning, reflects the kind of genuine hopes people may have had in the promise of someone embodying this *anima*ting truth. Augustine's disappointment at realizing the flaws found in his favorite ascetical home team, the Manichaeans, is summed up by him as follows: "I ought to have disgorged these men like vomit from my over laden system" (*Confessions* VII,2).[7]

But please notice, it is this sense of struggling to be victorious that prevails even amid such disappointing deception. Augustine's *De agone Christiano* begins, "The crown of victory is promised only to those who engage in the struggle."[8] In Augustine's particular case we can see both the attractiveness of the Manichaean militant asceticism and his disappointment at its ability to deceive good people. What stands out in Augustine is his struggling with God to know God. Early in the *Confessions*,

[7] St. Augustine, *Confessions*, trans. R.S. Pine-Coffin (London: Penguin Books, 1961).

[8] St. Augustine, *The Christian Combat (De agone Christiano)*, trans. Robert P. Russell, O.S.A., Fathers of the Church Series, vol. 4 (New York: CIMA Publishing Co., 1947) 315.

not exactly a work that we might think of as ascetical, but it is, Augustine asks the haunting question we too might ask:

> Why do you mean so much to me? Help me find words to explain. Why do I mean so much to you, that you should command me to love you? And if I fail to love you, you are angry and threaten me with great sorrow, as if not to love you were not sorrow enough in itself. Have pity on me and help me, O Lord my God. Tell me why you mean so much to me. *Whisper in my heart, I am here to save you*. Speak so that I may hear your words. My heart has ears ready to listen to you, Lord. Open them wide and *whisper in my heart, I am here to save you*. I shall hear your voice and make haste to clasp you to myself. Do not hide your face away from me, for I would gladly meet my death to see it, since not to see it would be death indeed. (I,5)

Here we find such an incredible mix of hardened ascetic ready to meet his death and at the same time that most tender longing of his heart—"whisper in my heart, I am here to save you."

Conclusion

As we have seen, asceticism animates a profound sense of the person arduously working toward some goal that requires virtuous living. It is a challenge not easily achieved but one that promises an incredible prize to those who endure to the end, disciplining the body and mind, conforming one to Christ. In a world beset with demiurges and world souls, primal battles of good and evil forces, both the uniqueness of Christ's Incarnation and the uniqueness of each individual person, which the Church magisterially named, offer a satisfying spiritual lifestyle. The self, with its integration and transcendence, relates the self to Christ and locates the self in this life of virtue, striving for the kingdom yet to come. It faces life confident of God's goodness and the unconquerable reality of Christ, the prototype of human perfection.

This ascetical spiritual integration has meaning in any life where the battle of good and evil is pronounced and a need is present to discipline one's life according to the example of Christ. For instance, asceticism offers an incredible spiritual *anima*tion for people facing recovery from addiction (chemical as well as behavioral) or the hellish struggle of divorce or cancer or AIDS. The battle of good over such evil requires the kind of asceticism that locates and relates a person in Christ, in Christ's love and in Christ's suffering. Many people today embrace an ascetical discipline due to very different battles, but still it is one of existential good and evil. If they were to be asked by Abbot Moses to name their objective, they might say "Justice" or "Equality" or "Peace" or "Life." They see aspects of their lives and know that only such discipline will change hearts and open minds. The ascetical integration tells the Christian in the midst of his or her struggle that in the end the victor's crown awaits. Someday "justice will rain down from the heavens," someday equality or peace or life itself will be the prize that unburdens all the pain, heals all the derision, and makes right all the wrongs.

Chapter Five

The Word Made Flesh, Dwelling Among Us: The Mystical Approach

Meet a Mystic: Catherine of Siena

Now that we have a sense of the ascetical way, we turn to the mystical. Again, it is valuable to meet a mystic in order to realize that he or she is not "airy fairy" as one friend said. Most Catholic mystics have been reformers—John of the Cross, Teresa of Avila, Meister Eckhart, and Catherine of Siena, to name a few. All of them are fascinating; however, I would like to look at my Dominican sister. Catherine of Siena offers us an example of the mystical tradition that many of us know. Born around 1347 in Siena, she was the youngest of twenty-three children. By her own choice, and only reluctantly on the part of her family, did she commit her life to virginity at an early age. Around 1364, at the age of seventeen, she became a Dominican tertiary. After an intense three-year period of austerity, she seemingly changed directions and embarked on a new sense of mission. In Siena a group of spiritual disciples had gathered around her. Her instruction and concerns gave rise to her writing a series of letters. She also began to take more of a role in the political life of her day.

Catherine was sent by the town of Florence to Avignon in order to negotiate a peace between the town and the pope, but this mission was not fully sincere on the part of Florence. A mystic who is engaged with the world is not exactly what most people think, and yet Christian mystics are drawn to the heart of creation in Christ. Later it is believed that Catherine even played a key role in Gregory XI's decision to return to Rome, though some scholars question this. Her letters give us an indication of her strong personality, and her greatest work, *The Dialogue*, was written three years before her death. It reflects the mystical sense of the mind's oneness with God and the mystery of the Incarnate Word. Catherine died in 1380. Her *Dialogue* gives a sense of her mystical animation of the Incarnation, and at this point in the work God is speaking to Catherine, providing the image of Christ that inspires her. It is this doctrine of the Incarnation that is captured in the dynamic image of a bridge. God says, "I told you that I have made a bridge of the Word, my only-begotten Son, and such is the truth. I want you to realize, my children, that by Adam's sinful disobedience the road was so broken up that no one could reach everlasting life. Since they had no share in the good for which I had created them, they did not give me the return of glory they owed me, and so my truth was not fulfilled."[1] Catherine's God desires our salvation as he continues asking, "What is this truth? That I had created them in my image and likeness so that they might have eternal life, sharing in my being and enjoying my supreme eternal tenderness and goodness. But because of their sin they never reached this goal and never fulfilled my truth, for sin closed heaven and the door of my mercy" (*Dialogue*, 58).

God explains the consequences of sin for humanity and his gift of the Incarnation, who is the bridge of the only Begotten Son. God next exhorts us, saying, "Open your mind's eye and you will see the blinded and the foolish, the imperfect, and the

---

[1] Catherine of Siena, *The Dialogue*, trans. Suzanne Noffke (New York: Paulist Press, 1980) 58–59.

perfect ones who follow me in truth. Then weep for the damnation of the foolish and be glad for the perfection of my beloved
children. Again, you will see the way of those who choose light
and the way of those who choose darkness." There really is
something amazing in the Incarnation if we but open ourselves
to its world of meaning. God continues, "But first I want you to
look at the bridge of my only-begotten Son, and notice its greatness. Look! It stretches from heaven to earth, joining the earth
of your humanity with the greatness of the Godhead. This is
what I mean when I say it stretches from heaven to earth—
through my union with humanity" (ibid., 59).

Amid a world of political change, ideas about governance,
dominance, and control forced alliances and allegiances of
people in society and in the Church. Catherine's noetic cosmology was that of knowing the world and God's will, God's plan
for humanity. It is in the Incarnation that Catherine finds meaning for her world, finds a way to spiritually animate her life. It
is also Catherine's sense of the Trinity, God working through
Christ "to undo great troubles," that shapes her spirituality. God
tells her to "open your mind's eye and you will see the blinded
and the foolish, the imperfect and the perfect who follow me in
truth." Catherine's noetic world is spiritually meaningful in its
ability to know beyond the apparent because true knowing is in
Christ—"through my union with humanity." It is this doctrinal
sense of God's bridging our human nature that enables Catherine
to see God rebuilding the broken roads of life, to see the meaning
of redemption.

Mystical Spirituality

In the previous chapter we saw how a dualistic cosmological
battle of good and evil, and an anthropology that saw human
existence as punishment for a primordial amnesia, was met by
the Christian doctrine's insistence on the uniqueness of the individual person created by God and the salvific role of Christ in
conquering the uncertainty of the cosmos. By way of anecdote,

we saw how Christian spiritual writers offered a sense of personal location and transcendence through ascetic disciplines that conformed them to the person of Christ through their practice of the virtuous life. Their own struggles took on meaning, and they imitated the witness of the martyrs in challenging mind and body, to run the good race and to win the victor's crown. In this chapter we find a different world that gave rise to another configuration of factors that demonstrate the mystical Christian spiritual life.

While I have discussed the Hellenic contribution to the West in its understanding of the soul, the same could be said for its partial influence in the East. The Arab *falasifas* devoted attention to Aristotle and what had come to be known as the two intellects of the soul. For Avicenna (980–1037) the last of the emanations was the human soul, temporarily united to a body. The active intellect, which for Plato came from the One as a knowing emanation, comes to be identified with God, and one of these primary incorporeal emanations is "Intellect."[2] To understand this "noetic world," as it is called, we have to think in terms of the process of knowing itself. This is not done conceptually nor in terms of anything that can be understood materially. Knowing is not like the workings of an automobile. Knowing is nonmaterial, not a thing. Consequently, no matter is involved in our knowing. There are brain functions but the mechanics of the mind are not the same as knowing. This amazing capacity to know captures the imagination.

For one of the Arab philosophers, Averroes (1126–98), the human soul was brought into being at birth and it ceased to be at death. Only when the thing exists can one say that its form is

---

[2] We may substitute God or the Mind of God, but for these authors there was the One, and the first noetic emanation of One is active intellect. The last noetic emanation is agent intellect, i.e., the human soul. One must be careful not to equate knowing with isolated bits of knowledge. For example, I can know a lot of facts (e.g., 2 + 2 = 4, 4 + 4 = 8, the times table). These are isolated facts, the body of knowledge in my head, but they are not knowing.

present. When a thing ceased to exist, the form ceased to exist as well. Therefore, when the body dies, the soul ceases to exist. For Averroes nothing could be considered part of the eternal. Both of these Muslim philosophers, Avicenna and Averroes, favored neoplatonic Aristotelianism, with its emphasis on the soul's power to know. This fascination with knowing comes to mark the noetic world we now study. "Noetic" means pertaining to the intellect, to knowing and the mind, a "world of under-standing." This noetic concern marks the mystical context as we will see.

These authors have taken from both Plato and Aristotle, mixed them together in different ways, but their aim was to try to understand this knowing, the noetic. The Muslim world's expansion to the Mediterranean, and the world of the Greeks, accounts for this philosophical influence upon their understanding of the soul. The Sufist tradition represents a more popularized version of the *falasifas*, while further to the East the great Oriental traditions of India and China were less burdened by Greek thought. Here the direct lines to Plato and Aristotle vanish, yet there remains an uncanny sense of the soul transported eastward via Gnostic and Manichaean routes.[3] Knowing this background helps us to appreciate what happened next.

Near the end of the twelfth century the philosophical writings of Aristotle, Avicenna, and Averroes hit what would have been medieval Europe's equivalent of the "best-seller list." These

---

[3] The *Upanishads* of India depict the individual souls and the world as generated by *Brahman*, the impersonal, pantheistic, world-soul. These souls entered bodies and were trapped in the world of illusion and suffering (*maya*), only to be freed by separation from the body and complete extinction of individuality through conscious knowing—the All (*Nirvana*). It is the purified soul that may return to the All and become lost in the All, while the souls of those who have died, not being purified, transmigrate to another body so as to undergo further purification. For the Chinese the soul is the rational principle *hun* that survives death and is the object of ancestor worship. This is the *yang* part of the soul while the passive, negative, earthly part (*yin*) is called *p'o*.

authors had a significant impact upon the thought of Europe, especially at the University of Paris. How this contributed to an understanding of the cosmos can be seen in the emergence of two different schools of thought on the soul's knowledge. One, the Augustinian-Bonaventuran school, held the unique immateriality of the soul and borrowed from the Jewish Spaniard Avicebron (ca. 1020–70) and his doctrine of "spiritual substance." With this doctrine the soul is understood as composed of spiritual matter and form. This would allow the soul to subsist on its own, to be an eternal entity independent of the body. The other school, the Aristotelian-Thomist tradition, accepted Aristotle's notion of hylomorphism. Aquinas insisted upon the metaphysical rule that matter and form be taken together. The human soul for this group is the form of the human body and apart neither one can properly exist. Thomas's concern was to guarantee that the individual existence of any person in this world was not simply accidental to a self-subsisting soul, which was Bonaventure's position. For Aquinas, bodily existence, in this world, was essential for the soul to exist. While Bonaventure wished to affirm the soul's "independence" from the body and its dependence on the divine will alone, as did the conservative Augustinianism of the time, Aquinas refused to abandon his conviction that the soul was the intrinsic principle of unity and required the materiality of this world and of the human body. However, Thomas needed to avoid the Averroestic reduction of the soul to its material body, and he needed to preserve the soul's capacity to transcend the limits of material embodiment. Thomas was caught between those who (1) advocated a plurality of forms in the human person (the soul's form plus the body's form), as with Bonaventure; and (2) those who reduced the form (soul) simply to the body's existing materiality. Thomas's goal was to preserve the essential unity of the person, requiring both the matter (*hyle*) and the form (*morphe*), body and soul, to be hylomorphically one in order for there to be an existing thing.

Both of these approaches meant that our knowledge of God must be affective and speculative. In other words, we know God by goodness and by truth, by our will and our intellect. The validity of both Bonaventure and Aquinas with their understandings of the soul made an impact on the thinking, praying, and practice of medieval Christianity. However, it was also a time when other forces bargained for models of the Christian life. Amid the orthodox mystical tradition was also to be found Oriental explanations of the soul that led to a dualistic opposition in Christian existence. The Church sought to clearly define an acceptable understanding of the soul, one consistent with a Christian anthropology. This scholastic interest in the metaphysical, and the University of Paris's politics over philosophy's independence at the university (Siger of Brabant), was matched by another popular reality far away from the university. Rather than focusing on the speculative questions of this noetic, that is, the mind's knowing, another mystical approach emerged, not in the university but in the monasteries and in the markets.

The question of the soul and the intellect had been present in many earlier thinkers like Gregory the Great (ca. 540–604) and Anselm of Canterbury (ca. 1033–1109). Fortunately the erroneous belief that the soul preexists the person had been definitively rejected by Leo the Great (d. 461). John Scotus Erigena (ca. 810–ca. 877) had introduced early medieval Europe to the neoplatonic thought of Dionysius the Pseudo-Areopagite (now known to have been a fifth-century Syrian monk). This literature, combined with the philosophical questions of the soul, gave rise to a renewed noetic interest among Christians, especially in Paris where Denis was believed to have been martyred. Consequently, the soul came to be understood within a tradition initiated by Bernard of Clairvaux (1090–1153) and Hugh of St. Victor (d. 1142). The disciples of these two men formed the Cistercian and Victorine schools, which stressed the affective character of the soul's union with God. In this "mystical" context the soul became the object of great religious and personal discussion. It alone became the key reality for many of these mystical writers.

This noetic cosmology, or a "world of understanding," linked human knowing with an almost divine potential. Not only did academic scholasticism fashion an understanding of knowing (epistemology) in the universities, but noetics, the art of knowing, also shaped the world in which people lived. Architecture, art, monasticism, mendicancy, civil and ecclesial structures, markets, monarchs, and popes defined minds and lands and nations and alliances. For example, the reforms of Gregory VII, the efforts at reconciling the schism with the East, the pilgrimages and crusades, the legal privileges given university masters, the lay religious movements such as the Beguines, and the establishment of professional guilds all bear witness to a world in which the importance of knowing was key. Knowing laws, crafts, one's enemies, one's rights, and God, all created a world engaged by this cosmological and anthropological mystery of knowing. In this age the macrocosm of God's mind and the microcosm of human illumination were truly one.

Earlier social reforms had established the Church as the "cyberspace" of its day, and the papacy was crucial to this noetic "world of understanding." With the death of Emperor Henry VI in 1197, Pope Innocent III settled the arbitrations over the successor to the Holy Roman Empire. In his bull *Venerabilem* Innocent also appropriated to the papacy the right to what was, for all practical purposes, final approval in the election of the emperor. In France, with the pope's reconciling Philip Augustus with his Danish wife Ingeborg; in England, with King John's subsequent submission to the pope after the king initially opposed the Holy See's naming of Stephen Langton Primate of England, Archbishop of Canterbury; as well as other such papal interventions in Scandinavia, the Iberian peninsula, and the Balkans; and in its patronage of the newly established Franciscans and Dominicans, the papacy enjoyed enormous ecclesial influence backed by the civil power of the French. Knowledge was power.

Christ Our Light and In His Light We See Light

This concern with right knowledge, or truth, was the hallmark of the times. It was only natural that a council called at the

Lateran sought to bring archbishops, bishops, abbots, superiors, and priors from all corners of the Latin Church, not to mention royal envoys sent by all the European princes. It was at this council that the bishops of southern France raised their concerns over the Albigenses. This offshoot of the Cathari sect shared the similar heretical beliefs of the Manichaeans.[4] It is important to note that the Cathari represented a significant challenge to a Catholic understanding of the world. Catharism came to Europe around the time of the Second Crusade (1147) and is believed to have been inspired by the Bogomils and the subsequent Catharist churches in Bulgaria. Kurt Rudolph[5] in his work on Gnosticism writes:

> The gnostic character of the Bogomilian doctrine is however clear: the history of the world is dominated by the struggle between the good God and the fallen Satanael who created the material world and man. Man's soul is derived from the good God and for its salvation from the evil body the "Word of God" (*logos*) was sent in the phantasmal body of Christ. (374)

So again we meet the Gnostic strands that we saw the ascetics confront. Here it undermines Christian doctrine. Notice below how the attitude toward standard ecclesial life is challenged:

> The hierarchy, the sacraments, the cult of the saints, the relics and the icons of the Church were rejected as inventions of Satan. Only the Lord's prayer and confession were retained. Reception into the community was by a "spiritual baptism"

---

[4] Manes of Persia (216–76) represents a blend of Persian and Indian as well as Gnostic influences. Manichaeanism was a dualistic view that understood existence in terms of a primeval conflict of light and dark. The devil (darkness) had trapped bits of light and imprisoned them in human beings. Jesus, Buddha, the Prophets, and Manes were sent to help free these bits of light through knowledge and a severe physical asceticism.

[5] Kurt Rudolph, *Gnosis: The Nature and History of An Ancient Religion*, trans. Robert McLachlan Wilson (Edinburgh: T&T Clark, 1983/1977).

which took the form of a laying on of hands. In the Bible the Old Testament was considered a work of Satan, while in the New Testament only the Gospel of St. John was considered to be an authentic proclamation of the true God. . . . [They] exerted particular power of attraction by their sharp criticism of the wealth and luxury of the . . . Church as well as of the wars and oppressions of the state. (ibid., 374–75)

In the thirteenth century the Church found herself again confronting the old dualism of Manichaeanism and Gnosticism.[6] While a noetic cosmology, or "world of understanding," promoted the knowing of the mind, the door was left open for a Gnostic anti-institutional movement with strong emphasis on poverty and celibacy, such as the Cathari. Such attacks needed to be addressed and, in a world of understanding, to be rightly understood. In response to newer forms of these heresies seen in the Albigenses, Pope Innocent III (1198–1216) summoned the Fourth Lateran Council (1215). His calling of this "twelfth ecumenical council" represents an expansion of the power (*plenitudo potestasis*) of the papacy into secular affairs. Note especially that this council strongly affirmed the unique creation of the human person both in body and spirit by the one Triune God who is beyond our fully knowing. They declared:

We firmly believe and profess without qualification that there is only one true God, eternal, immense, unchangeable, incomprehensible, omnipotent, and indescribable, the Father, the Son, and the Holy Spirit: three persons but one essence and a substance or nature that is wholly simple. The Father is from no one; the Son is from the Father only; and the Holy Spirit is

---

[6] For Gnosticism, as with Plato, there was a Supreme God (God) and a separate Creating God (Demiurge). The Demiurge immediately created and governed a world that opposed the truly spiritual. Gnosticism believed that for one reason or another little sparks of the divine spiritual stuff had entered into some creatures. These sparks or seeds were to be rescued by knowledge (*gnosis*), and such persons were "spiritual" while other less knowledgeable persons were "fleshly." Christ was the bearer of this liberating *gnosis*.

from both the Father and the Son equally. God has no beginning, he always is, and always will be; the Father is the pro-
genitor, the Son is being born, the Holy Spirit is proceeding;
they are all one substance, equally great, equally all-powerful,
equally eternal; they are the one and only principle of all
things—Creator of all things visible and invisible, spiritual
and corporeal, who, by his almighty power, from the very
beginning of time has created both orders of creatures in the
same way out of nothing, the spiritual or angelic world and
the corporeal or visible universe. (Denz. 428/TCT 335)

After eliminating any Gnostic notion of a dualistic God, the
council went on to define its Christian anthropology. This is
important in our study of spirituality. Just how is the soul to be
understood? The text continues:

And afterwards he formed the human creature, who in a way
belongs to both orders, as being composed of spirit and body.
For the devil and the other demons were created by God good
according to their nature, but they made themselves evil by
their own doing. As for humans, their sin was at the prompt-
ing of the devil. The Holy Trinity, indivisible according to its
essence, and distinct according to its personal properties, first
gave this teaching of salvation to the human race through
Moses and the prophets and its other servants, according to
a well-ordered disposition of time. (Denz. 428/TCT 335)

What we see in this Lateran definition is that the soul is uniquely
created by God. A closer reading also shows us something deeper
about human existence. Just as the demons were created good
according to their nature but chose to become evil, a similar
choice exists for the human person. Implied in this is the underlying moral dimension of human nature. This is extremely important! The human person combines the spiritual and corporeal
in a unique moral way. As a result, the mystical spirituality of
this period also entails a choice for the practical living out of the
Christian mystery. Mysticism and morality are related, just as
the Incarnation is related to our redemption.

Almost one hundred years after the Fourth Lateran Council, Clement V (1305–14) convened in Vienne, France, the fifteenth ecumenical council. It was meant to abolish the Knights Templar, as well as to address ecclesial reforms (the Inquisition, the universities at Paris, Oxford, Salamanca, and Bologna, as well as the Roman Court). The Council of Vienne (1312) also addressed the erroneous teachings of Peter John Olivi (1248–98) and the defiant Spiritual Franciscans. This council took place during the "French Babylonian captivity" of the Avignon papacy. So when King Philip IV of France thoughtfully appeared in that remote city one day in February of 1312 with an army, the council fathers suddenly found more sufficient reason to suppress the Knights Templar, handing over their fortunes in Paris to the king. However, the question of Franciscan poverty (the poverty of Christ controversy) was of less interest to the king. He left, and the council was able to formulate a clear condemnation of Olivi and his understanding of the soul's union with the body (among other propositions). As we see, a doctrine of the soul is taking shape. The Council of Vienne clearly defined the integrity of human existence, declaring the soul to be the essential form of the body:

> Furthermore, with the approval of the sacred council mentioned previously [Lateran], we condemn as erroneous and opposed to Catholic truth every doctrine and opinion that rashly asserts that the substance of the rational, intellectual soul is not truly and by its own nature the form of the human body, or that casts doubt on this matter. And we define that, whoever presumes to assert, defend, or stubbornly hold that the rational or intellectual soul is not of its own nature and essentially the form of the body, is to be considered a heretic. In this way the truth of the authentic faith is known to all and the path of error is blocked. (Denz. 481/TCT 336)

Here we see the council's adoption of Aquinas's notion of hylomorphism to explain the soul's relationship to the body. It was in 1278 that the Dominicans imposed Aquinas's teachings on the order. The Dominicans supported the Avignon papal court on the question of religious poverty for the friars, unlike the rigorist Franciscans who were influenced by the teachings of Olivi. One may surmise, if allowed to conjecture, that the Dominican definition of body and soul seemed, at the time, more compatible with papal politics. Even so, it also proved to be more compatible with Catholic doctrine in a world marked by noetic concerns.

Christian Mysticism: Union with God

Trying to marshal the great spiritual writers who chose this way of mystical integration into a few pages is extremely difficult. I wish to recall that this section is intended to offer a demonstration of the *anima*ting model by way of anecdote. Consequently my concern is how these mystical writers integrated life and doctrine in the reality of their individual lives, thereby animating Christian doctrine. It is, I'm afraid, a complicated task, which I am about to whittle down, offering the simplest rendition.

Mysticism is a widely used term in Christian and non-Christian religions. (While I cannot give a complete study of mysticism, the works of William Ernest Hocking and Baron Friedrich von Hügel[7] are commendable though dated.) In talking about a mystical integration I wish to distinguish three varieties: *visionary* mysticism, *affective* mysticism, and *speculative* mysticism. All three of these seek to take the noetic world, a "world of understanding," and bring a sense of a personal relation with the Triune God that has magisterial guidance. In so doing, they fostered authentic human existence directed toward union with God. Notice how each form of mysticism seeks fuller understanding of God and God's will for us.

---

[7] William Ernest Hocking, *The Meaning of God in Human Experience* (New Haven: Yale University Press, 1912/1963); and Baron Friedrich von Hügel, *The Mystical Element of Religion as Studied in Saint Catherine of Genoa and Her Friends* (London: J.M. Dent & Co., 1909).

VISIONARY MYSTICISM

Visionary mysticism offers a vivid image or dream, rich in metaphorical meaning. Very often the vision is prophetic. By that I mean that the vision speaks to a lived reality of the mystic and offers an instructive paradigm for Christian perfection. Hildegard of Bingen (1098–1179) is one of the great visionary mystics.[8] Sometime between 1146 and 1147 she wrote the renowned theologian of her day, Bernard of Clairvaux, about her visions:

> Father, I am greatly disturbed by a vision which has appeared to me through divine revelation, a vision seen not with my fleshly eyes but only in my spirit. . . . I have from earliest childhood seen great marvels which my tongue has no power to express but which the Spirit of God has taught me that I may believe. (27)[9]

She seeks Bernard's advice and his judgment on her visions. There is a need for the animating vision with its inner instruction to be part of the ecclesial community, its prayer, its Gospel. She continues:

> Through this vision which touches my heart and soul like a burning flame, teaching me profundities of meaning, I have an inward understanding of the Psalter, the Gospel, and other volumes. Nevertheless, I do not receive this knowledge in German. Indeed I have no formal training at all, for I know how to read only in the most elementary level, certainly with no deep analysis. But please give me your opinion in this matter, because I am untaught and untrained in exterior material, but am only taught inwardly, in my spirit. (*Letters*, 28)

Hildegard, amid a world of noetic concerns, finds in her inner dreams and vision an instruction beyond her abilities and seeks

---

[8] Margaret Ebner (1291–1351) is another similar visionary mystic.

[9] *The Letters of Hildegard of Bingen*, vol. 1, trans. Joseph Baird and Radd Ehrman (Oxford: OUP, 1994).

(and in fact receives) endorsement from the magisterial voice of her day, the great reformer of Clairvaux.

Living about three centuries after Hildegard, another visionary mystic, Dame Julian of Norwich (ca. 1342–after 1416), recounts a similar inner understanding of her visions. In her *Showings*, "The Long Text," she explains this inner noetic sense of her visions:

> The secrets of the revelation were deeply hidden in this mysterious example; and despite this I saw and understood that every showing is full of secrets. And therefore I must now tell of three attributes through which I have been somewhat consoled.
>
> The first is the beginning of the teaching which I understood from it at the time. The second is the inward instruction which I have understood from it since. The third is all the whole revelation from the beginning to the end, which our Lord God of his goodness freely and often brings before the eyes of my understanding.[10]

There is integration of the world through a noetic knowing that seeks inner understanding and finds it through the vivid images that speak to these writers. One aspect not clear from these texts but present in their writings is the desire to understand these visions in light of the mystery of the Trinity. Whereas the ascetics turned to the magisterial doctrine of the incarnate Christ, these mystics turn to the more sophisticated metaphysical notion of the Trinity, itself incomprehensible mystery, an understanding beyond understanding.

AFFECTIVE MYSTICISM

Affective mysticism, often called bridal mysticism, found integration in this noetic world with an inner sense of divine love that comes from the soul's union with God, especially

---

[10] Julian of Norwich, *Showings*, trans. Edmund Colledge and James Walsh (New York: Paulist Press, 1978) 269.

through one's will or love. What is significant with the affective mystics is their sense of giving direction or instruction to others in this process of perfection. Again, the difficult task of anecdotal demonstration must reduce to a few morsels what clearly is a feast. However, we can see the integrative elements present in these affective mystical writers.

In "prologues," a common device used to introduce their works, we find a means to characterize these works. Again, my purpose is to demonstrate their animating life. These affective mystics integrated the noetic world of knowing by dwelling upon the heart's capacity to know the object of its love, which is Christ or the Triune God.

Jan van Ruusbroec (1293–1381), the great Flemish bridal mystic, stressed the union that is found in human nature due to the Incarnation. In his prologue to "The Spiritual Espousal" he tells his readers of the noetic call, or as he puts it, "Christian Truth" concerning our call:

> Now Christ, the Master of Truth, says "See the Bridegroom comes, go out to meet him." In these words Christ our love teaches us four things. In the first he gives us a command when he says "See." Those who remain blind ignore this command, they are all damned. In the next word he tells us what we shall see, that is the coming of the Bridegroom. The third time he teaches us and commands what we should do when he says, "go out." In the fourth word when he says "meet him," he makes us aware of the purpose of our labors and our life, that is the loving meeting with our Bridegroom. (104)[11]

Ruusbroec's integration is one of the human heart being instructed by Christ in the very truth of this encounter of the heart with the love of Christ. Or notice the affection with which another male bridal mystic and English hermit, Richard Rolle (ca. 1300–1349), begins his *Ego Dormio*:

---

[11] Jan van Ruusbroec, *Werken*, "Die Geestelike Brulocht," my translation (Tielt: 1944).

You who desire love, [open your ears] and hear love. In the
Song of Love I find the expression . . . "I sleep but my heart
is awake." Great love is demonstrated by someone who is
never half hearted in loving, but unremittingly, whether standing, sitting, walking or [performing any other activity], is
constantly meditating on his love, and frequently even dream-
ing of it. Because I love [you] I am courting you in order to
have you exactly as I would wish—not for myself, but for my
lord. I want to become [a] go-between to lead you to the bed
of the one who has set you up and paid for you, Christ, son
of the king of heaven, because he is eager to [marry] you if
you are willing to give him your love. (133)[12]

For these affective mystics, it is in this loving relation to Christ
that one reaches an animating integration. It is a knowing in the
heart that is instructed by Christ. The biblical texts provide a
guide, and what becomes thin is the clear need for the ecclesial
community. Oftentimes this will be addressed through their
sense of the sacraments, but the theme that integrates is Christ
and the heart's love instructed by Christ.

SPECULATIVE MYSTICISM

With the speculative mystics we see that the noetic world is
integrated by a sense of the soul's intellectual union beyond
image and language. "Speculum" is Latin for mirror, and this
phenomenon fascinated the medievals. How can the image be
both in the source and in the mirror? How can God be both the
source and in us? Perhaps the greatest example of such a mystic
is found in Meister Eckhart (ca. 1260–ca. 1328). It is noetic knowing that is without distinction that arises from our contemplating
the wonder of human nature itself, especially in the nobility of
the human intellect. In one of the Meister's instructional works,
"Of the Nobleman," he writes:

[12] Richard Rolle, "Ego Dormio," *The English Writings*, trans. Rosamund
Allen (New York: Paulist Press, 1988).

> Our Lord says in the gospel, "A nobleman went out into a far
> country to obtain for himself a kingdom and returned" (Luke
> 19:12). Our Lord teaches us in these words how noble man
> has been created in his nature, and how divine that is which
> he can attain by grace, and also how man should attain to it.
> And in these words much of holy scripture is touched upon.[13]

Eckhart next explains human nature and the importance of the
inner person. He discusses various stages of perfection, coming
to the sixth and final stage, saying:

> The sixth stage is when the man becomes free of images and
> is transformed into the image of God's everlastingness and
> has attained to a complete and perfect oblivion of this transient
> life in time, and has been drawn and wholly changed into a
> divine image and has become God's child. Truly, there is no
> higher stage than this, and there is in it eternal repose and
> blessedness, for the end of the inner man and of the new man
> is eternal life. (*Essential Sermons*, 242)

For Eckhart, speculative mysticism is an intellectual negation of
concepts in order to attain such purity of soul that one is changed
into a divine image.

Angela of Foligno (ca. 1248–1309), who is better known as a
visionary mystic but serves to illustrate the blending of these
categories, offers another dimension of the speculative mystics.
In her "Instruction 29" she tells us it is knowledge of self that
brings us to knowledge of God. Unlike Eckhart's speculative
mysticism, which is apophatic (that is, by absence), Angela's
mysticism is self-knowledge as a kind of contrast to knowledge
of God.

---

[13] Meister Eckhart, *The Essential Sermons, Commentaries, Treatises, and Defense*,
trans. Edmund Colledge and Bernard McGinn (New York: Paulist Press,
1981) 240.

Knowledge of God presupposes knowledge of self in the following manner: One must consider and see who is the offended, and then consider and see who is the offender. From the insight derived from the second consideration, one is granted grace upon grace, vision upon vision, light upon light. And from these, one begins to attain knowledge of God.[14]

While briefly treated, it is true that the speculative mystics provide an integration of the noetic context through contemplating human knowledge. This brings one to know one's limits in simple union (Eckhart) or perfect love (Angela of Foligno).

Conclusion

Again, I wish to stress that my purpose has not been a full treatment of the mystics but to demonstrate that this mystical integration confronts a world whose cosmology is noetic, the world of the *nous* (knowing) and its anthropology. This anthropology is built on the noetic capacity of the human person to know and the power of such knowledge. The Church's magisterial instruction of this life context sought to retain the uniqueness of bodily human existence and the soul's necessary relation to that unique existence. However, there exists this ineffable wonder of human knowledge of the Trinity that promotes the kind of mystical fascination concerning the soul's illumination and union with God.

Mystical integration is best understood in relation to a noetic life context that pushes human knowledge to its very limits. With this understanding of mysticism we see that mystics may not be so rare as many think. The worlds of science, mathematics, physics, ecology, computer technology—all of these seem to be contextual settings for mystics. Philosophers, psychologists, and sociologists who seek understanding also face this same noetic

[14] Angela of Foligno, *Complete Works*, trans. Paul Lachance (New York: Paulist Press, 1993) 290.

world, this "world of understanding." The mystic integrates life and doctrine by locating a person in the wonder of what is beyond the limits of our knowing and the known. Yet one remains very much in relation to some knowable reality, some object worth knowing but never completely known. Doctrinally, Christian mysticism sees this knowing as an incredible and indescribable union with the one who has created us and who is our destiny, the Triune God.

As a spiritual lifestyle it offers an integration of a noetic world, a "world of understanding." Once mysticism is stripped of the unfair bizarre characterization, we recognize that our world is inhabited by more mystics than we think. A person working in research and development, a parent who is awed by the wonder of his child, a worker who is caught up on a project, or any seeker of truth awed by its faceted beauty—all these are very likely closet mystics. In fact, I find children are natural mystics, integrating their noetic world of knowing in very common visions, affections, and speculations. Their world of imagination integrates the limits of their knowledge in the questions, and more questions, and more questions. In our study of spirituality we do mysticism a disservice if we only look at the bizarre and do not enter that eerie boundary between known and unknown, a "world of understanding." As a Christian spiritual lifestyle the Church's magisterial teaching, its doctrines on Person and Trinity, serve to guide such mystical integration. Without this doctrinal factor, this type of integration can easily run wild.

Chapter Six

God's Beauty Fills the Earth:
The Aesthetical Approach

Meet an Aesthetic: Ignatius of Loyola

Now that we have met two spiritual representatives of different approaches, it's probably helpful to review them. In using the approach to spirituality that I am advocating, we are able to appreciate how a particular life context is met and integrated by a particular doctrine. In a real sense, the spiritual writer is doing theology in the lived reality of his or her spirituality. This helps us to look at a particular spirituality with a fuller scope, to see the breadth of its genius. So, when we met Maximus the Confessor, we realized that the ascetical approach faces a world of struggle, marked by a battle between good and evil. The ascetic finds a deepened sense of the Incarnation, the struggle of humanity against very difficult circumstances. Asceticism allows one to meet the soul of one's being by seeing the value of discipline, discipleship. In the Incarnation of Jesus Christ the ascetic finds the mystery of one's own humanity. In a similar way, when we met a mystic like Catherine of Siena, we saw the need to face a world of understanding. The mystic seeks to know the meaning of the image of God, to see this indwelling abiding in one's very soul. Here is where the mystic explores the doctrine of the Trinity, its unity and distinction, its personal sense of the reality of God, its abiding presence, and its ultimate promise for each one of us. The doctrine of the Trinity guides spiritual integration, for it is the threefold mystery of the Trinity that calls the mystic to seek true understanding. Knowing this truth, the dynamic relationship of the Trinity of persons and unity of Godhead, allows the mystic to integrate his or her world.

Now we turn our attention to yet another approach, the aesthetical tradition. This, I acknowledge, is an unusual word, but the concept is important. We often hear the word "aesthetic" when we think of art and a sense of the beautiful. Someone who is "aesthetic" has a sense of the beautiful, a genuine love of beauty. In another sense an aesthetic is in touch with the pure emotion and sensation as opposed to a pure intellectuality. Such awareness, such sense of the beauty that surrounds us, such a feeling for the good that is seen in the beauty of life, also can be seen as marking an approach to spirituality. Suggestive of this aesthetic tradition is the personality of Ignatius of Loyola. Born in 1491, he lived at a time of emerging kingdoms, with monarchs who were consolidating their powers (Henry VIII of England, Francis I of France, and Charles I of Spain, who also became Holy Roman Emperor Charles V). It was in the midst of Spain's political boom in Europe, as well as overseas in Peru and Mexico, that Ignatius lived and founded his society. In 1521 his right leg was injured by a French cannonball in the siege at Pamploma. The French took him to Loyola, where during his recovery his life took a dramatic turn. It was there that he read the Dominican Jacobus de Varagine's work on the saints, *Legenda aurea*, and the Carthusian Ludolph of Saxony's work *Vita Jesu Christi*. In 1522–23 he went to Manresa, and it was during this period that he was inspired to write his *Spiritual Exercises*. Soon after this, he made a pilgrimage to Jerusalem before entering university studies in 1524, first at Barcelona, then Alcala, and finally at Salamanca.

In 1534 Ignatius began a vowed life with six companions, and in 1540 the papal bull *Regimi militantis ecclesiae* formally established the Society of Jesus. This "company" sought to foster religious zeal amid the realities of the Protestant Reformation. His *Spiritual Exercises* reflect Ignatius's own spiritual development, but in an age of Humanist interests it provided a primary text for a Catholic aesthetic. What do I mean by this? Ignatius's *Exercises* involve the person in a reflection upon his or her life and the day's events. This is the examination of conscience that guides an awareness of God's will in my life. Ignatius offers the person making the retreat twenty annotations, which are a kind of directed do-it-yourself.

In his sixteenth annotation Ignatius takes this honest self-appraisal and instructs people to seek the opposite of what they find to be out of order in themselves:

> Thus, if someone is inclined to pursue and hold on to an office or benefice, not for the honor and glory of God our Lord or for the spiritual welfare of souls, but rather for one's own temporal advantage and interests, one should try to bring oneself to desire the opposite. One should make earnest prayers and other spiritual exercises and ask God our Lord for the contrary; that is, to have no desire for this office or benefice or anything else unless his Divine Majesty has put proper order into those desires, and has by this means so changed one's earlier attachment that one's motive in desiring or holding on to one thing rather than another will now be only the service, honor, and glory of his Divine Majesty.[1]

Notice how important it is for the personal, honest self-appraisal, self-awareness. Ignatius lived in a Humanist age where the "knowing subject" provides certainty. How one achieves spiritual integration demands an honesty that reveals the truth or beauty of the person. However, this is only achieved through a process of critical self-reflection, of an awareness of the good, the bad, and the ugly in us. Rather than focusing on the metaphysical that we saw with the mystic, or the existential focus we

---

[1] Ignatius of Loyola, *The Spiritual Exercises and Selected Works*, ed. George E. Ganss (New York: Paulist Press, 1991) 125.

saw with the ascetic, this aesthetic spirituality sees the subjective self as a critical starting point. Knowledge of self really is the beginning of true knowledge. But this must not end up in isolation. For Ignatius, the purpose of the *Exercises* is to do them with a director, a kind of mentor or guide. It is this aesthetic appreciation of the person's life and struggles that gives aesthetical spirituality its unusual focus. Notice what Ignatius advises in the nineteenth annotation:

> A person who is involved in public affairs or pressing occupations but educated or intelligent may take an hour and a half each day to perform the Exercises. To such a one the director can explain the end for which human beings are created. Then he or she can explain for half an hour the particular examen, the general examen, and the method of confessing and receiving the Eucharist. For three days this exercitant should make a meditation for an hour each morning on the first, second, and third sins; then for another three days at the same hour the meditation on the punishment corresponding to sins. During these three meditations the ten Additional Directives should be given the exercitant. For the mysteries of Christ our Lord this exercitant should follow the same procedure as is explained below and at length throughout the Exercises themselves. (*Spiritual Exercises*, 126–27)

For Ignatius, unlike Luther, his spirituality focused on the individual but held the individual in relationship with the Church, as the Body of Christ. You see how the sacramental life of the Church is placed within this aesthetical awareness through the sacraments of reconciliation and Eucharist. It prevents the personal side from being divorced from the communal dimension. An honest acceptance of one's sinfulness and an ongoing reflection on its evil and its consequences foster a genuine self-awareness. It is from this vantage point that one grows in spiritual awareness. The aesthetic approach shares the ascetical sense of discipline, but here it is a discipline of self—self-control, self-restraint, self-discovery. It is this solitude of self that opens the door to spiritual growth and integration. Ignatius tells us in the twentieth annotation the purpose of such solitude.

> By moving out of one's place of residence and taking a differ-ent house or room where one can live in the greatest possible solitude, and thus be free to attend Mass and Vespers daily without fear of hindrance from acquaintance. Three principal advantages flow from this seclusion, among many others. First, by withdrawing from friends and acquaintances and likewise from various activities that are not well ordered, in order to serve and praise God our Lord, we gain much merit in the eyes of his Divine Majesty. Second, by being secluded in this way and not having our mind divided among many matters, but by concentrating instead all our attention on one alone, namely, the service of our Creator and our own spiritual progress, we enjoy a freer use of our natural faculties for seek-ing diligently what we so ardently desire. Third, the more we keep ourselves alone and secluded, the more fit do we make ourselves to approach and attain to our Creator and Lord; and the nearer we come to him in this way, the more do we dispose ourselves to receive graces and gifts from his divine and supreme goodness. (ibid., 127–28)

This aesthetical appreciation of the true self enables one to be open to the divine will, to order one's own will to such service. Ignatius's Humanist cosmology, its sense of the self and human creativity, brought him to spiritually integrating life in Christian aesthetics. One comes to a true appreciation of the self, of one's intent, in order to fulfill one's human call. Ignatius's spirituality is animated by his sense of the doctrine of creation, God's divine majesty and our "createdness" as human beings. We human beings have been given a genius to manifest God's glory. Through the discipline of the *Spiritual Exercises*, along with a director and ninety minutes a day, a person can discover "the end for which human beings are created." It is in the life of the Church, in "attending Mass and Vespers daily," that one discov-ers the beauty of God's majesty—"to receive graces and gifts from his divine and supreme good."

Aesthetic Spirituality

Traditionally "aesthetics" is associated with appreciating objects of art, as we saw. But what if the human person is seen as that object? In that case we may address aesthetical spirituality as the beauty of one's life. There are two additional aspects that make this approach credible: epistemology (theories of knowing) and ethics (theories of virtuous living). These provide the "primary colors" for this aesthetic spirituality, which unfortunately has been traditionally called post-Reformation spirituality. While the ascetical tradition faced a world of moral struggle, and the mystical faced a world of understanding, this aesthetical tradition faced an age marked by human genius. Art, science, exploration, politics, and religion were seen as the work of human hands. While I intend to cover five hundred years packed with change and development, even fifty years during these centuries is a difficult task. The reason for my taking this roughly five-hundred-year span is that it falls between two key councils. This helps us to see how the doctrines, or lack of clear doctrines, forced a spirituality that was more homespun, traditional, and pietistic.

A Changing World

In the centuries following the Council of Vienne (1312), Western "culture" had undergone a significant transformation. No longer was the classical view of antiquity the one that secured the center of society. Rather, the stage was set for a changing world and a reform in the Church that would essentially fall along nationalistic lines. In 1438 the Gallicanism of the French Church sought greater autonomy from the papacy in its "Pragmatic Sanction of Bourges." The marriage of Ferdinand V to Isabella united the Iberian kingdoms of Aragon and Castile in 1469. Furthermore, Ferdinand's expulsion of the Moors and the Jews (1492), his zealous use of the "Inquisition," and his ambition for power shifted "Catholic" loyalties. Now the papacy would look to Spain for political support. Henry VIII had ascended to the throne of England in 1509; in Europe the remnant of the Holy Roman Empire was fragmenting into independent nations.

Socially the development of commerce was altering the nature of the cities, making them centers of banking and trade, with great economic and political power. Columbus's voyage had completely changed Europe's definition of the world. The Great Schism in the West (1378–1417), and the rise of the conciliar movement, challenged the notion of supreme authority in the Church. In 1409, the cardinals, independent of the pope, convoked a council at Pisa in the hopes of ending the Western Schism. Sadly it did anything but that. Both popes (Gregory XII and the antipope Benedict XIII) convoked rival councils, so the cardinals' gambit was doomed to fail. Their deposing the two existing popes and electing Cardinal Peter Philargi (1339–1410) as Pope Alexander V only made for three claimants to the chair of Peter in a world where temporal, princely power was on the rise. The Church was changing as the Christian West began to encounter strange cultures and different-looking people, even questioning their humanity or "ensoulment." As one might guess, the events of these centuries were a far cry from the noetic world of the previous period. The years, roughly covering 1517—when Luther (1483–1546) attacked the "enterprising" Tetzel (1465–1519) for selling indulgences—up to the Council of Trent (1545–63), saw a turbulent period in Europe.

In addition, this period saw the rise and spread of Humanist philosophies. Marsilio Ficino's (1433–99) *Theologica Platonica* (1482) saw the universe as a hierarchical system (God, Angelic Mind, Soul, Quality, Body), and the human person was understood as pivotal. Human life was viewed as an interior ascent of the soul toward God. The immortal soul was studied in terms of its journey to immortality. But perhaps the lasting impact left by Ficino was his notion of "Platonic love," which rippled throughout the popular literature of the sixteenth century. This sense of the secular world and its growing body of literature and art is critical. We are dealing with a period that exploded the old way of thinking and challenged past, time-honored traditions. Three movements—the Renaissance, the Enlightenment, and Romanticism—serve to illustrate this change in human self-understanding and understanding of the soul. I warn the reader that there is a lot here, so go slowly, allow yourself time to digest the ideas.

THE RENAISSANCE

The Italian Renaissance gave rise to several challenges to a Catholic understanding of the soul. Pietro Pomponazzi's (1462–1525) *Tractatus de immortalitate animae* denied Aristotle's teaching on the immortality of the soul; instead he held it to be a material form. Bernardino Telesio (1509–88) stressed the empirical sciences, stopping short of a complete biological analysis of the soul. He was convinced that a super-added form (*forma superaddita*) informed the body and spirit, which was capable of union with God. And a disciple of Telesio, the troubled renegade Dominican Giordano Bruno (1548–1600), whose naturalism and pantheistic mysticism saw the soul reabsorbed into the "God Reality" that was synonymous with the "Universe Reality," further complicated an understanding of the soul. There was in the air a strong anti-Aristotelian movement that opted for a more Platonic naturalism.

The 1600s also saw a shift wherein the Renaissance thinkers were replaced by the mechanical philosophy of Thomas Hobbes (1588–1679), René Descartes (1596–1650), and Isaac Newton (1642–1727); the empiricism of John Locke (1632–1704); the rationalism of Benedict Spinoza (1632–77) and Gottfried Wilhelm Leibniz (1646–1716). Like a great executioner the movements of the 1600s were preparing the block, and the axe was readied to sever the last link of the body politic from its head, the Church. Of course it will not be until the eighteenth century when the guillotine (1789) is introduced by the French and Napoleon re-establishes Catholicism in France but in a very French manner. This "rebirth" soon needed guidance, which would come forth in the Enlightenment.

THE ENLIGHTENMENT

The Enlightenment can be characterized as the crowning of reason as the absolute monarch of human life. This period extended from the early seventeenth century to the beginning of the nineteenth century. René Descartes represents the start of a methodical abandonment of scholastic thought and the heady embrace of rationalistic, empiricist, and idealist philosophies. The standard or slogan *cogito ergo sum* of Cartesian thought subjected everything to its criterion for truth, "clear and distinct ideas." For the Cartesians, all organic reality had to obey mechanistic laws, and this included the human body. The soul, as life principle, could not fit this requirement for a mechanistic understanding. Descartes therefore reduced the soul to an immaterial unextended being, located in the pineal gland, communicating with the body through the brain and the nervous system. By imposing this mechanistic view upon bodily behavior, there arose the belief that human behavior was in response to stimulated mechanics. "Thinking," that one undeniable fact of the *cogito*, became equated with the soul. Like a fine machine, the body ran according to rules of nature, carrying within it the *res cogitans* (the thinking thing) and the *res cogitate* (the things thought).

What is important for us to note and acknowledge about this period is that philosophy outran religion in defining the cosmos. Galileo Galilei (1564–1642) and others stood against the Church, holding human reason as their testimony to the divine. No longer did the noetic of humbly knowing the divine mind guide the period, but the art of human knowledge, extracted from the created world, now made human reason an equal to the Creator. Leibniz rejected the intercausal relations of the mechanistic view and advocated the soul as a base unit (monad) possessing within itself the principle of all its changes, while the body was an aggregate of inferior monads and both soul and body ran side by side in preestablished harmony yet remained independent. The illustration Leibniz used for this was that of two clocks set side by side, syncopated so that the pendulums simultaneously swung with one another, making these "clocks" run in perfect harmony. The "body clock" functioned with the "soul clock" but both remained independent. This harmony, a syncopation of body and soul, promoted a dualism of causes. The soul acted according to final causes, while the body acted according to the laws of efficient causes. The monad was the only thing that was taken to be of concern because within it was all the potential for change.[2] For Leibniz, thinking is the monad's only activity wherein it comes to knowledge of itself, and of God as its final cause. In this life we humans function according to the laws of efficient causes. Benedict Spinoza (1632–77) offered an understanding that reduced reality to one thing (Monism). There was no difference between body and soul. The soul is one with the cosmos and our thinking is an activity of the divine mind. While the empiricists like John Locke (1632–1704), George Berkeley (1685–1753), and David Hume (1711–76) were not Monists, they did see the soul in terms of a perceiving active being that thinks because it experiences. These bundles of experience Hume called "self." Notice that in these last authors we move from a language of soul to a language of the self. This will have a lasting impact on spirituality.

The Idealism of Immanuel Kant (1724–1804), called transcendentalism or transcendental Idealism, sought to disrupt the

---

[2] Within the Aristotelian notion of causality there were four causes of a thing; two of them were intrinsic to the thing itself, two of them extrinsic. The formal and material causes were intrinsic to the thing. The efficient or the "doing" cause and the final, or "end product," which were external to the thing. For example, if I want to build a house, intrinsic to the house that I will eventually build is its own material cause and its own formal cause. To get to the house that I want to build, I have to do the building. My making it, my working on it, my using these physical materials is the efficient cause. I'm efficiently working on it. The "blueprint" of what I finally want done is not the thing done, the thing I was after all along. Everything that is promoted or caused is because I wanted a house; the ending up with the built house itself is the final cause. The thing as finished in its final state gives cause as to why I ever began working on the thing, and is said to be the final cause.

rationalistic metaphysics of his time. The soul was one of the ultimate synthetic principles of reason. Other such principles for Kant were "World" and "God." If I might try to simplify this, human beings need certain synthesizing principles that serve to pool our thoughts together. They are like "harbors of ideas." The soul is one of those harbors of thinking in which we synthesize our ideas. We can't prove that the soul exists, but for Kant, the notion that there is a soul was a synthetic principle, an *a priori* notion. We can only talk of existing because there is a soul. Kant believed that there was no way to prove that there is or isn't a God, there is or isn't a soul, there is or isn't a world. Rather than trying to explain these notions, one must simply accept them as *a priori*, synthetic principles. As such, any attempt to prove the soul's substance, simplicity, or eternity is an error in reasoning. "Soul" is the synthetic principle for knowing one's practical and moral purpose. Ethical consciousness demands that there be an immortal soul. Kant's major works[3] had a profound impact upon German and European thought for the next two centuries. We need to appreciate the cultural context that pervaded this period.

Another German, Georg Wilhelm Friedrich Hegel (1770–1831), challenged the notion of an immortal soul with his famous dialectic method. His operative notion was perpetual becoming through a synthetic resolution of antithetical propositions: the famous thesis, antithesis, synthesis formula. For Hegel, a thesis gives rise to an opposing anti-thesis, and in this dialectical struggle there emerges a new syn-thesis (a kind of intellectual survival of the fittest). Traditionally, one should recall, the absolute world was the world of perfection or the world of finished being, while the imperfect world was the world of becoming. For Hegel, this wasn't the case. He dismissed the notion of the world of perfection (which includes the notion of an absolute, perfect God). For him, what remains is this world of becoming.

---

[3] *Critique of Pure Reason* (1781/87), *Critique of Practical Reason* (1788), and *Critique of Judgment* (1789–93).

This notion of perpetual becoming is possible because of an ongoing synthetic resolution of antithetical propositions. This dynamic warrants repeating—a thesis struggles against an antithesis and out of this struggle rises a synthesis that is the new thesis against which an antithesis opposes and thus struggles again, and again, etc. This does not allow for an enduring soul but one that must ascend to self-consciousness and ultimately to universal self-consciousness (*Geist*).[4] Undoubtedly Hegel's most significant work was his *Phenomenology of Spirit*, printed in 1807. However, for Hegel, "spirit" or *Geist* meant mind or consciousness. "Soul" for Hegel was that endless becoming of consciousness. You can see how this contributed to a notion of spirituality as personal consciousness. One element of German Idealism deserves particular attention for providing a transition between Kant and Hegel, as well as for its impact beyond philosophy—and that element is Romanticism.

ROMANTICISM

This modern period clearly placed the human subject in the middle of it all and began to free one from any unquestioned religious authority. However, the price demanded was a shift in authority, not its loss. Authority was now transferred from religion into the hands of the sovereign, or the state and its civic religion. The cosmology and anthropology of the Enlightenment became tethered to human reason, but this sacrificed transcendence, which was now sought in the movement called Romanticism.

Romanticism fostered a greater emphasis on the human imagination with an optimistic belief in its immediate comprehension. Art expressed emotion. And aesthetics, fed by the thoughts of Voltaire, Rousseau, and others, gave rise to a civic religion that

---

[4] "Consciousness" is always rising up higher and higher (thesis/antithesis/synthesis), so it actualizes all the potentials of human self-consciousness and even devours any notion of universal consciousness.

met the needs of an increasingly secular Humanism. The progress of science and the eighteenth century's cosmopolitan sense of travel and social organization all created an atmosphere critical of Roman Christianity. The historian Henri Daniel-Rops writes:

> In order to explain the rapid progress of nonconformist ideas we must add yet another fact of paramount importance: whereas the rebellious clique included a large number of highly talented men, there was very little talent among those who defended religion and the establishment. In the days of Pascal, Racine, and Bossuet genius was on the side of faith. It was on the opposite side in the days of Rousseau and Voltaire.[5]

Romanticism in art, music, and even politics held court where once theology had been queen. Beauty, that is, one's experience of beauty, was not only the anthropological ground of the day but it was also an entire cosmology, as math and music, science and society found the beautiful in the optimistic human capacity for progress. This movement, which included such thinkers as Friedrich Ernst Daniel Schleiermacher (1768–1834) and Friedrich Wilhelm Joseph von Schelling (1775–1854), covers the period between 1775 and 1815. Like German Idealism, it held that all reality was ultimately spiritual, but spiritual taken as the Absolute Spirit (the Over-Mind) and knowable by the human spirit (mind). For the Romanticists this Absolute Spirit was not understood as a moralist (Kant) nor as a logician (Hegel) but as an artist, infinitely creative, endlessly evolving. Nature played a key role in this process of manifesting the Absolute Spirit. While human beings were seen as even higher manifestations of Absolute Spirit, humanity was also the place where Absolute Spirit became conscious of its own creative work. Nature, the human person, and Absolute Spirit (their "God") were all taken as part of the same evolving creative process, acting out Absolute

---

[5] Henri Daniel-Rops, *The Church in the Eighteenth Century*, trans. John Warrington (London: Dent & Sons, 1964) 43.

Spirit's coming into consciousness of itself in nature and human consciousness. This exaggerated interest in nature inspired artists and poets with an intense and naive effort to capture the phenomenon of nature. It emphasized feeling, imagination, and sentiment over reason. One can easily see how this influenced and still influences some notions of spirituality.

Christian Aestheticism: God in Spirit and in Truth

What is very striking as we turn to the doctrinal teaching during this time is its thinness. During these three centuries Catholic teaching was weak or ineffective in the face of strong popular movements. During the sixteenth to eighteenth centuries, only two ecumenical councils were convened—Lateran V (1512) and Trent (1545–47, 1551–52, 1562–63). This is surprising given the number of changes in the world over these centuries. However, this gap calls attention to the accelerating pace of social change and the Roman Church's increased isolation from political power.

LATERAN V

It was against this backdrop of papal isolation that Pope Julius II (1503–13, b. 1443) convened the fifth council at Lateran. Its main purpose was to invalidate the uncertain legitimacy of the Council of Pisa. Interestingly, it did not address the concerns and issues of the Reformation. With regards to the soul, the key concept of our survey, Lateran restated the teaching put forth at the Council of Vienne. It stressed that each person has his or her own unique, distinct soul. Notice the language in the council's decree, how it labors with a classical cosmology:

> We regretfully mention that recently the sower of cockle, the ancient enemy of the human race, has dared to oversow the Lord's field and to give increase to some dangerous errors, which have always been disapproved by the faithful. These errors concern the nature of the rational soul especially—for

instance, that the soul is mortal or that there is only one soul
for all people. We condemn those who raise doubts about this
matter. For the soul is not only truly, of its own nature, and
essentially the form of the human body, as is stated in the
canon of our predecessor Pope Clement V of happy memory,
and published in the (general) Council of Vienne, but also it
is immortal and, corresponding to the number of bodies into
which it is infused, is capable of being multiplied in individuals, is actually multiplied, and must be multiplied. (Denz.
738/TCT 345)

Importantly, the Fifth Lateran Council opposed any notion of
there being a cosmic world soul in which our "human souls"
are partakers. Rather, soul is multiple, uniquely infused in each
individual human being, and it is the essential form of the
human body. Even to this day notions of a world soul surface
in spirituality, and it is rightly challenged by Catholic teaching.
Why? Because a world soul denies the uniqueness of each individual soul and each soul's ultimate destiny and responsibility.

TRENT

Trent, begun in 1545, roughly thirty years after Lateran V,
is crucial because it established the ideals of the Counter-
Reformation. It was a revival or reform of the Catholic Church
and took fifteen years of political negotiations before it could be
held, which indicates how the Church was now being defined
in light of a new political world order. Sessions 1 through 7 were
held at Trent (1545–47) but it moved to Bologna for session 8,
given the tensions between Pope Paul III and Charles V. After a
four-year interruption, phase two (sessions 9–14) was again at
Trent (1551–52) under Pope Julius III, but it was suspended when
the princes revolted against Charles V. Ten years and two popes
later, the third phase (sessions 15–25) was held at Trent (1562–63)
without interruption under Pope Paul IV.

The council clearly intended to address the realities of Protestantism, even though some had hoped it would work toward

conciliation with the Protestants. What is remarkable is that from Lateran V, which reiterated the Council of Vienne, through Trent there was no teaching on the soul, no Christian anthropology to help face the uncertainties of the time. Not until Vatican I in 1869, over three hundred years later, do we see magisterial teaching from the Church. This means that through the three historical periods we examined, the Renaissance, the Enlightenment, and into Romanticism, the Catholic Church did not give conciliar teaching to the women and men of this period. This is remarkable—close to three hundred years without an ecumenical council addressing serious questions about human nature.

VATICAN I

It is not until the nineteenth century that we see the kind of "dogmatic" pronouncements on the soul that have come to characterize modern magisterial teaching. I include Vatican I in this present discussion to help illustrate how the Catholic Church arrested its magisterial role in spiritual development and inadvertently fostered an aesthetics of personal, private spiritual life of perfection.

The Modern realities differed greatly from those of the Reformation. The Church was pressed to debate its theological and religious convictions in a world grown hostile and alien to that of the twelfth and thirteenth centuries at the zenith of papal power and authority. Science, with its empiricism and materialism, made savage waste of appeals to divine law or apostolic succession. Human inquiry began devouring the Sacred Scriptures as nothing more than one archaeological artifact among many others, as one form of literature to be studied the way one might study the *Iliad* or the works of Shakespeare. The Church no longer occupied a central place in world politics; in fact, it was not even considered a player, and so the prospect of an ecumenical council was a nonevent for the governments of the world. However, among "Roman Catholics" a great debate was churning over religious (papal) authority. The Ultramontane movement advocated the centralization of power in the papal Curia against the movement for greater national or diocesan autonomy. In nations with a Catholic majority such as Spain and Italy papal authority was not a problem; the real struggle was for those Protestant nations with a Roman Catholic minority that looked to Rome for support, and those pluralistic democracies such as the United States that needed greater local autonomy to adapt Roman Catholicism in accord with "democratic life."

Perhaps as a result of poor administration and communication, the *Syllabus of Errors* (1864) set out eighty condemned theses. It attempted to tackle three hundred years of neglect with an overhaul of errors and took on what were seen to be false doctrines. The division of the *Syllabus* is set forth under ten headings:

1. Pantheism, Naturalism and Absolute Rationalism

2. Moderate Rationalism

3. Indifferentism and Latitudinarism

4. Socialism, Communism, Secret Societies, Bible Societies, and Liberal-clerical Societies

5. The Church and Its Rights

6. Civil Society and Its Relation to the Church

7. Natural and Christian Ethics

8. Christian Marriage

9. The Temporal Power of the Pope

10. Modern Liberalism

These ten headings catalogue the uneasy relationship of the Church with the Modern state's erroneous ways. Papal infallibility and the primacy of the pope were taken to be the only true course on this sea of tempestuous errors. Pius IX (1846–78, b. 1792) was more than willing to fulfill that role. Perhaps it was his forced flight from Italy in 1848 and his unheeded appeal to the Catholic European heads of government for the restoration of the Papal States, or his final return to Rome aided by the French army, that convinced the initially open pontiff to greater caution with political liberalism, which he now saw as threatening the Church. Even so, his pontificate, which surpassed the legendary twenty-five-year reign of St. Peter, not only defined the immaculate conception (1854) as doctrine but also ushered into existence the modern papacy with its powerful Curia.

Notice how this effort to clearly address serious issues stands in contrast to the previous three centuries, a serious neglect on the part of magisterial instruction. The First Vatican Council was held in St. Peter's Basilica and was announced five years in advance by Pius IX on December 6, 1864. It was the first council held in the age of enlightened democratic nations, and so it followed the parliamentary rule set forth in the apostolic letter *Multiplices inter* (December 2, 1869). The process involved the advance work of commissions that were brought to the general congregations where these schemata were debated. Only six of the fifty-one preliminary schemata came before the council. From the start, the debates centered on the issue of Catholic faith and the harsh eighteen-chapter schema, which most of the council members criticized as too technical, too negative, too apodictic, and not pastoral. The American bishops were quite vocal not only on this first draft of the Dogmatic Constitution on the Catholic Faith (*Dei Filius*) but also on papal infallibility. Peter Richard Kenrick (1806–96), archbishop of St. Louis (bishop 1843, raised to archbishop in 1847), led the minority party in opposing papal infallibility. The Canadian archbishop of Halifax, Nova Scotia, Thomas Louis Connolly (1815–76; arch. 1859), also sided with Kenrick.[6] To illustrate this emerging understanding of the human soul, Augustin Verot (1805-1876), bishop of Savannah, also in Kenrick's camp, asked for the council to condemn theories that denied that black and Indian peoples had souls.

---

[6] A total of fifty-four absented themselves from the final vote for the doctrinal constitution *Pastor Aeternus* on papal infallibility rather than vote *non placet*, which reflects the strain of the council.

This first phase of debate lasted from December 1869 until January 10, 1870. A shorter and more pastoral version was discussed from March 18 until April 24, winning a majority vote of 667 to 0. It is in this dogmatic constitution that we find clear doctrinal pronouncements on God's creation of the human soul. Chapter 1 of *Dei Filius* emphasized its apostolic, catholic, conciliar, and parliamentary authority:

> Now, therefore, with the bishops of the whole world being associated with Us and concurring in judgment, assembled for this ecumenical council by Our authority in the Holy Spirit, We have determined to profess and declare the saving doctrine of Christ from this Chair of Peter in view of all people. We do so, relying on the word of God in writing and in tradition, as we have received it from the Catholic Church, religiously guarded and authentically explained. All opposing errors We proscribe and condemn by the authority given to Us by God. (Denz. 1781/TCT 354)

After professing faith in the one living and true God who is distinct from the universe, the document proceeds to oppose various errors in modern thought:

> In order to manifest his perfection through the benefits which he bestows on creatures—not to intensify his happiness nor to acquire any perfection—this one and only true God, by his goodness and "almighty power" and by a completely free decision, "from the very beginning of time has created both orders of creatures in the same way out of nothing, the spiritual or angelic world and the corporeal or visible universe. And afterwards he formed the human creature, who in a way belongs to both orders, as the human being is composed of spirit and Body." (ibid.)

Again the council stresses what we see as the constant Catholic understanding of human existence having a spiritual as well as temporal integrity. However, the council next insists that God still providentially guides and governs:

Furthermore, by his providence God watches over and governs all the things that he made, reaching from end to end with might and disposing all things with gentleness (*Wisdom 8:1*). For "all things are naked and open to God's eyes" (*Heb. 4:13*), even those things that are going to occur by the free action of creatures. (Denz. 1783–84/TCT 356–57)

Following chapter 1 there are several canons that condemn specific errors, again the necessity to redress the centuries of neglect:

1. If anyone denies that there is one true God, creator and lord of things visible and invisible: let that one be anathema.

2. If anyone dares to assert that nothing exists except matter: let that one be anathema.

3. If anyone says that God and all things possess one and the same substance and essence: let that one be anathema.

4. If anyone says that finite things, both corporeal and spiritual, or at least spiritual, emanated from the divine substance; or that the divine essence becomes all things by a manifestation or evolution of itself; or, finally, that God is universal or indefinite being, which by determining itself makes up the universe which is diversified into genera, species, and individuals: let that one be anathema.

5. If anyone does not admit that the world and everything in it, both spiritual and material, have been produced in their entire substance by God out of nothing; or says that God did not create with a will free from all necessity, but that he created necessarily, just as he necessarily loves himself; or denies that the world was made for the glory of God: let that one be anathema. (Denz. 1801–5/TCT 358–62)

Notice how materialism and pantheism receive the strongest condemnation both in general and in specific forms. In this particular case the intended authors of these beliefs were Georg

Hermes (1775–1831) and Anton Günther (1783–1863). The former was strongly influenced by Kant, the latter by Hegel, and both men had sizeable followers after their respective deaths. Günther's followers affiliated with the Old Catholics (Declaration of Utrecht 1889), and Hermesianism was condemned at Vatican I. So the question we are left with is what kind of spiritual integration arises when there is an absence of magisterial direction.

The Grandeur of God

The aesthetic tradition can be characterized by its emphasis upon the beauty of human experience that is faithful to goodness. Catholic spiritual writers, who were both people of their time and sought to be faithful to the Church in very uncertain times, advanced a program of spiritual exercises and personal devotion. The saintly models held up are representative of true loyalty to the Church, and yet very much part of the Humanism of their time. Catholic spirituality in this tradition reflects an aesthetics of the one holy Roman Catholic Church. In Catholic nations, like Spain and Bavaria, this aesthetic shaped the whole social fabric. In non-Catholic nations, it provided a sense of identity in the face of oppression and political discrimination (Ultramontane). The Catholic aestheticism differs from Romanticism by clearly connecting the freedom and optimism of the Humanists with the institutional realities of the Catholic Church.[7] While I have covered almost five hundred years, it is a period of remarkable change, impacting both cosmology and anthropology, during which the Catholic Church's magisterial role *de facto* was diminished.

While an anecdotal approach has shortcomings, it does serve to demonstrate this aesthetic tradition that appears when certain

[7] For a point of comparison see how American Transcendentalists intended to bring the individual to the universal spirit or oversoul found in all of nature and human nature as well.

factors are present. During this period we find very limited formal magisterial guidance from the Church as to the ultimate meaning of human existence. A person needed to exercise a certain personal choice to believe, and this meant personal guidance. Catholic countries were governed by increasingly independent-minded rulers who had more of a national sense of the Catholic Church and who were pleased with limited doctrinal interference. In Protestant countries, the Catholic minority increasingly sought support and guidance from their Church. Both of these factors inadvertently shaped a domestic Catholic aesthetic of spiritual direction and devotion that was personal, socially acceptable, and intellectually satisfying.

While Martin Luther promoted a reform of Christianity opposed to Roman papist controls, his contemporary—eight years younger than Luther and dying ten years after him—Ignatius of Loyola (1491–1556), and the enterprisingly named Society of Jesus, labored for "the propagation of the faith." Ignatius's *Spiritual Exercises* was completed in 1541, five years before Luther's death, and has had more impact on Catholic spirituality than any other single work, apart from the Bible. The aesthetics of these exercises met the Humanist needs of the time with its lengthy attention to the individual (four weeks of personal exercises) and its use of one's creative imagination in prayer. Yet, while centered on the individual, it is clearly tied to the Catholic Church. In fact, one section is titled "Rules for thinking, judging, and feeling with the Church."[8] The *Exercises* begins with an explanation that appeals to personal direction and private devotion:

> By the term Spiritual Exercises we mean every method of examination of conscience, meditation, contemplation, vocal or mental prayer, and other spiritual activities, such as will be mentioned later. For just as taking a walk, traveling on foot, and running are physical exercises, so is the name spiritual

[8] *Spiritual Exercises*, Ganss, ed., 211.

exercises given to any means of preparing and disposing our soul to rid itself of all its disordered affections and then, after their removal, of seeking and finding God's will in the ordering of our life for the salvation of our soul. (121)

Here we see spirituality as an aesthetic of life, "seeking and finding God's will" so that one can reasonably order one's life. This kind of spirituality met the tension between one's personal experience and one's fidelity to the Catholic Church. This is in marked contrast to the Protestantism of Luther's stress on the priesthood of all the baptized and his attack of the Romanist "three walls."

Unfortunately, or fortunately, the kind of magisterial guidance that people sought was no longer provided by a classical sense of Christianity. People looked for guidance in their newfound freedom. This need was met in the kind of spiritual direction set forth by Ignatius but given a personal warmth in the seventeenth century with the influence of Pierre Cardinal de Bérulle (1575–1629). An explosion of Catholic writers emerged due to the inspiration of this French noble clergyman whom Pope Urban VIII described as the *Apostolus Verbi Incarnati*. Bérulle promoted a humane spirituality focused on Christ as God-made-man. In his famous *Discourse on the Nature and Grandeur of Jesus* (1623) Bérulle poetically praises humanity in a tone quite at home with his times:

Oh humanity, divinely subsistent, divinely living, divinely active. You are worthy in this divine and infinite attribute that you possess. You are infinitely, most infinitely worthy of ruling all that has been created or could be created. Endowed with superior power, you are worthy of commanding all that can be commanded. For even brute nature is sensitive to your commands. We see this in the tempests, winds, and storms, and other raging elements, which have obeyed you.[9]

[9] *Bérulle and the French School*, ed. William Thompson, trans. Lowell Glendon (New York: Paulist Press, 1989) 120.

Again it is important to keep in mind that this is during that three-hundred-year gap after Trent. An aesthetic tradition seemed to set souls on fire, chiefly in the most liberal country of France. Francis de Sales (1567–1662), Jane de Chantal (1572–1641), Vincent de Paul (1581–1660), Louise de Marillac (1591–1660), and Jean-Jacques Olier (1608–57) were all rough contemporaries of Bérulle who founded religious communities that still exist today (Salesians, Visitations, Vincentians, Daughters of Charity, and Sulpicians, respectively). Clearly the aesthetic tradition is closely guided by missionary religious communities whose direction, often through correspondence, reached lay women and men.

The written correspondence of people such as Francis de Sales or Jane de Chantal offers a glimpse into this aesthetic of personal experience and intimate trust of directee shown to director. Jane writes one directee, Noël Brulart, the court-appointed French ambassador to Spain and Rome:

> It is perhaps out of place to tell you this, Sir, but I find myself ready to speak to you in all simplicity and confidence, as if I had had the honor of meeting you and knowing you personally, so much have you opened my heart by the kindness, frankness, and trust with which you have been pleased to speak to me.[10]

Notice too how she affectionately writes her own brother Andre Frémont, archbishop of Bourges:

> I thank and praise our good God for the blessing He is pleased to have given us through the exchange made possible by our perfect friendship; for I assure you that if my letters enkindle in you the flame of love for the supreme Good, your very dear letters arouse the same feelings in me and make me wish more and more that our hearts be totally and constantly united to the good pleasure of God. (*Letters*, 204–5)

---

[10] Francis de Sales, Jane de Chantal, *Letters of Spiritual Direction*, trans. Péronne Marie Thibert (New York: Paulist Press, 1988) 187.

The "art" or aesthetics of correspondence in the spiritual life has long been a reality, as seen in Paul's Pastoral Epistles. However, this resurgence in the seventeenth century seems part of an aesthetical expression of the times, growing in the many sons and daughters of the new religious communities.

In the eighteenth century this aesthetical tradition is enhanced by people like Alphonsus Liguori (1696–1787) and Paul of the Cross (1694–1775). Their founding of the Redemptorists and the Passionists would continue the Catholic aesthetical tradition along private and personal, yet very ecclesial, lines still a century before Vatican I. Not only in their spiritual direction and correspondence but in prayers, preaching, missions, and devotions, we see an aesthetical tradition making sense of a Humanist world in the beauty of personally experiencing the good.

What is a striking feature is that due to a lack of dogmatic teaching, magisterial instruction is, inadvertently perhaps, distributed out to religious women and men providing an intimacy with the divine in specific devotions and religious personalities. One needs to take caution with this aesthetical tradition. When the institutional Church is muted on magisterial instruction, aesthetic integration becomes increasingly relegated to the private sphere of individual spiritual direction to the detriment of a more communal dimension. "My" aesthetic spirituality runs the risk of overpersonalizing religion and God. This can be seen in the following prayer by Jean-Jacques Olier, founder of the Sulpicians and seventeenth-century defender of Trent:

> My God how adorable you are in this spectacle of nature! My God, you are much more beautiful and more wondrous in yourself than concealed in these beautiful things! O my God, how happy I would be if my faith and your holy light allowed me to see what you are beneath them. . . . The Universe, my God, and even a thousand universes together could not represent you. . . . It is fitting, O my All, that you caused your creatures to speak perceptibly to our eyes and ears, proclaiming what you are and teaching us something of what you keep hidden in yourself. . . . O Fullness of Being, how perfect you

are! How pure and holy you are! (Thompson, *Bérulle and the French School*, 280–81)

Its sense is free, personal, and private. God truly is my God, with no mention of the Trinity. Delighting in the beauty of creation, it is closer to an aesthetics of the naturalist. As God and religion are gathered into my experience there is a greater need for magisterial instruction, which is often seen as an intrusion.

This aesthetical tradition confronts a tension between the anthropology and cosmology that promote greater religious freedom from Rome and center on the personal role of spiritual direction. In a spiritual tradition where external authority is removed or muted, it naturally turns to personal and private means of authentication. While this historical period was taken with the beauty of nature in art and music,[11] a Catholic aesthetic turned toward a very guided appreciation of humanity and beauty. The clergy, especially religious order clergy, fulfilled the magisterial role locally, at the parochial and personal levels.

Conclusion

It seems that this particular aesthetical tradition is still in the process of defining itself along a continuum. It thrives where there is a fundamental question as to the importance of one's personal experience and the role of ecclesial authority in those experiences. Many women and men, religious and lay, continue to find an aesthetic of spiritual direction crucial in their integration of doctrine and life. Here is where we need to encourage the charism of those directors, but we must acknowledge a twofold need. On the one hand, the professional qualifications and love for the Church on the part of the director are critical. On the

---

[11] In the world of music alone, both the Baroque composers such as Pachelbel, Scarlatti, Vivaldi, Bach, Handel; and Romantics like Paganini, Rossini, Schubert, Berlioz, Chopin, Liszt, Wagner, Verdi all flourished, to name but a few better known names.

other hand, the magisterial importance of the institutional Church failed to see that her doctrinal understanding of creation and redemption addressed these new challenges. Notice how so many spiritual books and articles today struggle to name creation and redemption. In Latin America or among feminists of the high tech world or among womanists of the emerging world, for traditionalist Catholics of Opus Dei or liberal Catholics in Call To Action, this aesthetical tradition is happening on the personal level. Aesthetic authority is now found in the personal integrity of my praxis, how one practices the faith.

The danger that I see is an increasing selectivity on both the right and the left to become decoupage Catholics—cutting, pasting, and shellacking what individuals feel to be acceptable snippets of the Roman Catholic tradition for their plaques. Yet, spiritual direction is the Catholic form of aesthetics in which one is able to appreciate his or her personal experience, guided by the friendly presence of a sympathetic director. Recall even Ignatius, in the *Exercises*, advised:

> That both the giver and the receiver of the Spiritual Exercises may be of greater help and benefit to each other, it should be presupposed that every good Christian ought to be more eager to put a good interpretation on a neighbor's statement than to condemn it. Further, if one cannot interpret it favorably, one should ask how the other means it. If that meaning is wrong, one should correct the person with love, and if this is not enough, one should search out every appropriate means through which, by understanding the statement in a good way, it may be saved. (129)

This aesthetical integration requires women and men of personal integrity to be witnesses to an authority that is ecclesial or communal. This is a key struggle we see especially today in aesthetical forms of spirituality.

Chapter Seven

Lord, When Did We See You in Need?
The Social-Critical Approach

Meet a Social-Criticalist: Mother Teresa of Calcutta

As we look at this last approach we come closest to the life context with which we are most familiar. It is easier to sense how the particular realities of our age influenced a form of spirituality that confronts a world of social concern. What is also significant of this period is that we see a strong magisterial voice on the part of the Church. This is in contrast to the previous approach, so amid the social uncertainties there is a strong voice that names the doctrinal concerns and guides our way to integrating our life. There are numerous examples of this spirituality, but one person stands out because of her unlikely prospects. She was probably one of the most universally known figures in her life and spoke to Christians and non-Christians alike, to young and old, to rich and poor.

This amazing individual was Mother Teresa of Calcutta, who represents an example of this social-critical tradition. Born August 26, 1910, in the Albanian town of Skopje, she was called Agnes Gonxha Bojaxhiu. Agnes was the last of three children born to Nikola Bojaxhiu and his wife Dranafile Bernai. As a young girl she was influenced by the Croatian Jesuits in her parish, and they recommended that she join the missionary sisters of Loreta. Agnes first went to Rathfarnham, Ireland, for her religious formation before being sent to Calcutta at the age of nineteen. For the next twenty years of her life she would teach history and geography at Loreta Entally. This was a private high school for girls in a comfortable neighborhood outside of Calcutta. At twenty-seven Agnes completed her religious vows, becoming Sr. Teresa, and continued to teach. Later she became principal of the high school. It was in her late thirties that Sr. Teresa became increasingly aware of conditions for the poor in India. This was a profound moment that shaped her sense of self. As she traveled by train to Darjeeling, amidst the throngs of poor women and men, she came to the conclusion that would change her spirituality forever. She recounted later that she knew she was to leave the convent and help the poor while living among them. The struggles with her superiors over this new-found calling were difficult ones, but in 1948 she was given permission to leave her assignment at Loreta Entally and work among the sick. One day, upon finding a woman dying in the streets, her flesh being eaten by rats, Teresa took her in and cared for her until she died. Some of Teresa's former students offered support, and one or two eventually joined in her work along with others who formed the Missionaries of Charity (approved within the archdiocese of Calcutta and later made a pontifical congregation under the jurisdiction of Rome in 1950).

One of their first houses was on the abandoned temple grounds of Kali, where they brought those dying and left in the streets, so that they might die with dignity. To devout Hindus, her use of the temple of Kali was a profanation. One report tells how the Hindu priests went to the Calcutta police commissioner, demanding her eviction. After he went to the temple and saw the Missionaries of Charity, their work with the dying, their feeding the hungry, he went back to those who demanded her eviction. He told them, "I promised I would get that woman out of here, and I shall. But, listen to me, I shall not get her out of this place before you get your mothers and sisters to do the work these nuns are doing. In the temple you have a Goddess in stone; here you have a living Goddess."[1]

Not only were her sisters reaching out to the poor in India but in 1975, after visiting New York, Sr. Teresa established a community in the ghetto, acknowledging the neo-poverty of the developed world. Often maligned by radical groups for her simple faith and loyalty to the Catholic Church, she represents greater social action than many bourgeois causes can claim. In 1979 she was awarded the Nobel Peace Prize and continued, in spite of declining health, to lead the Missionaries of Charity around the world.

Mother Teresa beautifully captures this social-criticalist spirituality's sense of service to the Gospel. In *Contemplative in the Heart of the World*, which was compiled by Br. Angelo Devananda Scolozzi, Teresa is reported to say:

> Total surrender consists in giving ourselves completely to God. Why must we give ourselves fully to God? Because God has given Himself to us. If God, who owes nothing to us, is ready to impart to us no less than Himself, shall we answer with just a fraction of ourselves? To give ourselves fully to God is a means of receiving God Himself. I live for God and give up my own self and in this way induce God to live for me. Therefore, to possess God, we must allow Him to possess our souls. How poor we would be if God had not given us the power of giving ourselves to Him! How rich we are now! How easy it is to conquer God! We give ourselves to God; then God is ours and there can be nothing more ours than God. The money with which God repays our surrender is Himself.[2]

[1] Edward LeJoly, *Servant of Love* (New York: Harper & Row, 1977) 58.

[2] *Mother Teresa, Contemplative in the Heart of the World*, compiled by Angelo Devananda Scolozzi (Ann Arbor, MI: Servant Books, 1985) 57–58.

You find in her spiritual integration a sense of the doctrine of Christ's suffering in his passion and death. The social doctrine of the Church is tied to a teaching about salvation called soteriology. But just as we saw in Catherine of Siena a sense of the Incarnation, we see in Teresa a remarkable, intimate solidarity in this suffering:

> Our vocation is the conviction that "I belong to Him." Because I belong to Him, He must be free to use me. I must surrender completely. When we look at his cross, we understand his love. His head is bent down to kiss us. His hands are extended to embrace us. His heart is wide open to receive us. This is what we have to be in the world today. We, too, must have our head bent down to our people—to the school where we are teaching or the sick and dying destitute that we are helping. This is Jesus in distressing disguise. Whether in the school or in the slum, it is the same Jesus. He said very clearly, "You did it to me. I was hungry . . . I was naked . . . I was homeless." Let us not make the mistake of thinking that the hunger is only for a piece of bread. The hunger of today is much greater; it is a hunger for love, to be wanted, to be cared for, to be somebody. (*Contemplative in the Heart*, 58–59)

Mother Teresa's context, her world and understanding of humanity, is marked by the reality of the poor. They bring her to the reality of suffering and there to face the doctrine of Christ's passion and death. Theodicy is the question of human suffering and God's place in that suffering. This question set in motion a life-changing reality for this woman. She left the posh world of a privileged school for young girls to *help the poor while living among them*. In a world of stark poverty and wealth, of consumerism, of materialism, Mother Teresa found spiritual integration in knowing God's economy and our place in God's generous love. Her faith allowed her to shift away from self-centered possessiveness to realize that we are God's most cherished possession—"I belong to Him."

Social-Critical Spirituality

It is difficult to evaluate the events closest to home, and this final tradition is no exception. Here we meet the optimistic exuberance of the nineteenth century and the horrific disillusionment of the twentieth. Just as our last tradition faced the promise of the Renaissance and the newfound liberties of the Enlightenment, so, too, this tradition faces the promise of Modernity and the second fall from paradise, only vaguely understood as Post-Modernity. It is this later period that holds our interest, for as the previous tradition turned to an aesthetic cosmology and anthropology, we see the nineteenth and twentieth centuries addicted to a notion of human progress.

As colonial powers sewed the world together in a patchwork of power around the globe, diplomacy and equality began to unravel. The high-minded ideals that supported their colonialization began to rupture. Despots and dictators followed the revolutionary examples set earlier in Europe, forcing the same unrest among previously docile and dominated colonies. The two world wars represent a wound in political life, as deep as the Reform had been for ecclesial life. Authority, which had come to be seen as part of the sovereign's or state's rule, was recast according to a politics of power and dominance (and now terrorism). On behalf of the people ruled, insurgents and revolutionaries inaugurated an escalating culture of violence in China, India, and the Philippines, finally reaching its most unfortunate expression in the Second World War. Even a postwar world relied on an artificial peace that existed because of a "balance of power."

With the collapse of Communism and the end of the Soviet bloc the world saw that the drive to acquire power proved to be too costly for the players. Even the price of Modernity may be too great as it experiences its own internal critique in what has been called "Post-Modernism." Modernity put its faith in science, or more correctly scientific technology, and the belief that research brought advances that meant a kind of Darwinian social evolution. Let us briefly sketch this context and its understanding of humanity that gave rise to the social-critical tradition.

Modernity

Again I wish to warn the reader that what follows is fairly packed and will take some refreshing of one's memory, or some additional reading. Part of this context is precisely this overwhelming flood of ideas on humanity. With the close of the nineteenth century and the dawn of the twentieth, philosophy fell upon a new "modern era" of science and industrialization. Edmund Husserl (1859–1938) developed his descriptive philosophy known as phenomenology, which sought to analyze the subjective processes of human inquiry. By transcendental reflection one critically brackets out the phenomenon to attain the transcendental ego, the source of meaning for all objective phenomena. It is this psycho-physical "I" that serves as the "soul," split between lived events and the transcendent ego. Maurice Merleau-Ponty (1908–61) replaced the notion of soul with a similar subjective source of meaning in the unfolding of the body-subject. For the neopositivists such as Bertrand Russell (1872–1970) the classical formulation of the soul was equated with nothing more than an expression of feeling, which asserts no empirical experience. Whereas the materialism of Karl Marx (1818–83) and Vladimir Ilyich Lenin (1870–1924) eliminated any "soul dimension" to the person, consciousness was seen only as a by-product of the brain.

For the existentialists, metaphysics was dead, and the only thing left was existence itself. Karl Jaspers (1883–1969) equated the archaic term "soul" with that being that stands against the totality of world-being (existence). Psychology and history, not metaphysics, provided the tools for his analysis. Gabriel Marcel (1889–1973) equated the soul with a quality of one's response to bodily being, while Jean-Paul Sartre (1905–80) saw no fixed essence or nature in the human person, or as the title to one of his works declared—*Being and Nothingness*. However, it is in the unique brand of existentialism fashioned by Martin Heidegger (1889–1967) that soul is retained as the sustaining principle that grounds true power, beauty, courage, authenticity, and creativity. Concern (*Sorge*) is the authenticating horizon for human existence, and dread (*Angst*), the fear of being at the edge of nothing-ness, compels one to the authenticating essence of concern, that is, care.

Post-Modernity

Modernity gave rise to an internal, self-critical reaction commonly called Post-Modernity. I wish to touch upon some of its pertinent aspects. The rather imprecise term of Post-Modernity suggests a reality after Modernity and a time prior to its own "coming of age," or self-identification. For as much as the Modern age did to capitalize on human potentiality, it has left us with a deep-seated mistrust of its fundamental suppositions. The aftermath of the Enlightenment and German Idealism, with its undaunted conviction that reason marches purposefully forward, has left us victims of its "Sherman-style" drive to the sea that burned everything in its wake. The great scientific advances in industry and technology are now choking the atmosphere and have inflicted new deadly diseases; the great economic and political experiments now reveal the physical oppression and economic exploitation required for their running; and even the great hope of human ingenuity has been exposed for the ideological biases it masks.

Hermeneutics is the study of interpreting texts, and what seems to mark this Post-Modern era was a hermeneutics of suspicion extracted from the ideas of Sigmund Freud (1856–1939), Karl Marx (1818–92), and Friedrich Nietzsche (1844–1900) by a generation dissatisfied and bent on tearing down (deconstructing) the presuppositions of the past. Writers such as Jacques Derrida (*Writing and Difference*, 1978), Emmanuel Levinas (*Existence and Existents*, 1978), and Michel Foucault (*Madness and Civilization: A History of Insanity in the Age of Reason*, 1965) have turned their critical tools upon the present age. Jürgen Habermas (*Theory and Practice*, 1973) and Hans Georg Gadamer (*Truth and Method*, 1975) have made significant contributions in their critical social analysis of human alienation and fear of otherness (alterity/difference);

while Mark C. Taylor (*Erring: A Postmodern A/theology*, 1987) and Don Cupitt (*Life Lines*, 1986) turned this hermeneutic of suspicion toward religion itself.

If you are feeling overwhelmed by the listing of these critical thinkers, you are sensing the challenge of this cultural context. Uncertainty and suspicion play havoc with our understanding humanity, especially something like the soul. As far as Post-Modernity's understanding of some idea even analogous to the "soul," it is difficult to state, since as you can see, all options are open and all options are equally valid. Perhaps more telling are the final lines from Cupitt's 1986 work:

> For, and here we come to the end of our windings, in effect we have said that it is only because there is no truth, and instead merely a plurality of truths, that we have been able to rehabilitate the spiritual life, as being a pilgrimage through a long series of truths. Furthermore, this pilgrimage has no great destination and is never complete, but merely passes out into scattering and endlessness. We read the New Testament as a story of the decentering and scattering of God, of Christ, and of the people of God: a story of diaspora. And in this long pilgrimage into diaspora, which we love and in which we find joy, lies the meaning of our life.[3]

This diaspora, alluding to the scattering of the Jews to countries outside of Palestine after the Babylonian captivity, has shaped and forged the present quest for spiritual integration. Unfortunately there seems to be such an emphasis on individual choice that doctrinal guidance is seen as suspect, limiting human freedom.

The Catholic aesthetic of spiritual direction, discussed in the previous chapter, sought to maintain the Humanist optimism of the personal in close association with magisterial instruction of a Roman Church that was remote or politically isolated.

---

[3] Don Cupitt, *Life Lines* (London: SCM Press, 1986) 214.

Catholics, in politics and in the press, were aware of the political and social necessity of their democratic involvement as citizens. Christian Churches, Catholic and Protestant, found increasing opposition from growing nationalist and secularist movements in democratic societies. Both the Catholic aesthetic of personal spiritual direction, especially by the clergy and religious, as well as the emergence of Christian Democratic movements, created a back door into politics for the Church. Facing the common enemy of secularism, Catholics and Protestants forged, through the Christian Democrats, critical associations, especially among workers, employers, the young, and women.

As citizens in democratic societies, believers faced the challenges of integrating their Christian principles into social and political life. The dangerous alternatives of Communism and socialism kept the Christian Churches united against the common enemy of secularism and atheism. Among Catholics the challenge of identifying a religious presence in the secular arena of the Modern state was crucial. The aim of the Christian Democratic movement, which began in Italy, was along personalist lines that emphasized the value of the person in human and moral life, possessing dignity, freedom, and responsibility.[4]

What stands out is that this Christian Democratic movement was able to work because of the individual freedoms and political liberalism won in Great Britain's Revolution of 1688, America's Revolution of 1776, and France's Revolution of 1789. The very liberties of the liberal state, which had ghettoized the Church, especially the Catholic Church, were now fast becoming the means for Christian political involvement. Michael Fogarty gives us a sense of the nuances Christian Democrats made when sleeping with the liberal state. Rather than try to capture his precision, I wish to quote him extensively:

[4] For examples see the personalism of Borden Parker Bowne, A. Seth Prizle-Pattison, and Maurice Blondel.

A Christian Democrat will criticize the liberal approach as too individualist, and as "humanist" in the sense of secularist. His own view, he would say, is "personalist" in the sense of bringing into account all the dimensions of personality; social as well as individual, supernatural (and therefore Church) as well as purely human. Christian Democrats share with socialists an appreciation of the importance and rights of the collectivity, and especially the State. But they hasten to add that they are not "collectivist" either, in the sense of over stressing the role of any particular social grouping, and notably that of the State. They are on the contrary "solidarist" in the sense of thinking always of collectivities as being at the service of the individual, not as superior to him. And they are "pluralist" or "federalist" in that they appreciate the community of all the peoples of the world, and try to mark out the functions and organizations appropriate to each and its rights and duties over the rest. The state takes its place as merely one, and not necessarily or always the most important, in a hierarchy of social groups. Christian Democrats are also conservative, in that they share with conservatives an appreciation of the time factor, of the difficulties of successful change, and of the importance of smooth continuous development. But they are convinced also of man's right and duty to advance towards mastering his environment by the power of his reason and will. They will stoutly deny that they are "traditionalist," in the sense of being particularly attached to the shape of things as it now is or once was.[5]

We can see that the Christian Democratic movement provided a Catholic political presence in society, but increasingly Catholics lived in two compartments, the world and the Church. The question for this social-critical tradition would be how the Church might bring these worlds together.

---

[5] Michael Fogarty, *Christian Democracy in Western Europe, 1820–1953* (London: Routledge, 1957) 17–18.

Christian Social-Criticalism:
Those Poor or Afflicted in Any Way

When John XXIII became Supreme Pontiff in 1958, many wondered how long this seventy-seven-year-old overweight Bishop of Rome would live. No one knew that in less than three months after being elected, he would have set in motion the plans for an ecumenical council that he hoped would bring a spiritual renewal to the life and mission of the Church, reconcile the divisions among Christians in the East as well as in the West, and bring the Church into the modern world and the needs of its day. The history of this council begun by John XXIII and concluded under Paul VI (1963–78, b. 1897) would take more space and deserve greater care than we are now free to devote to it. It is part of the living memory of many, and its heritage is still being lived. While the Second Vatican Council was undeniably an event for the Modern world, it is this Post-Modern world that strives to understand its intent for our day. Consequently, this present tradition of social-critical integration stretches from the apex of Modernity to the shifting reality of Post-Modernity, from the Industrial Revolution to our present day.

In our attention to the Church's key anthropological doctrine of the soul, we find that Vatican II has profoundly altered the Church's anti-Modernism and refashioned a greater fondness for the Modern world. Unlike its preceding Council there is no Dogmatic Constitution on the Catholic Faith, but a Dogmatic Constitution on the Church (*Lumen Gentium*, 1964), as well as a Pastoral Constitution on the Church in the Modern World (*Gaudium et Spes*, 1965). There are two further constitutions, one dogmatic treating divine revelation (*Dei Verbum*, 1965), the other, and first completed document of the council, was on sacred liturgy (*Sacrosanctum Concilium*, 1963). In addition to these four constitutions the council enacted nine decrees and three declarations. It was a council providentially gifted with numerous progressive cardinals such as Bernard Alfrink of Utrecht, Augustin Bea of the Pontifical Biblical Commission, Leo Joseph Seunens of Brussels, Albert Meyer of Chicago, Joseph Ritter of St. Louis, and Lawrence Shehan of Baltimore that helped move the Church into the twentieth century.

If we wish to understand the soul in these council documents, we must turn to the Pastoral Constitution on the Church in the Modern World (*Gaudium et Spes*). The language of body and soul plays a secondary, metaphorical role, having been surmounted by the more pastoral and acceptable phrase "dignity of the human person." It is my opinion that no document of this council begins more beautifully. "The joy and hope, the grief and anguish of the men of our time, especially of those who are poor or afflicted in any way, are the joy and hope, the grief and anguish of the followers of Christ as well."[6]

Its preface and introduction sketch out the world situation, bringing us to part 1, "The Church and Man's Vocation." The first chapter is devoted to the dignity of the human person, and in paragraph fourteen the soul and body are seen as part of the essential nature of the human person:

> Man, though made of body and soul, is a unity. Through his very bodily condition he sums up in himself the elements of the material world. Through him they are thus brought to their highest perfection and can raise their voice in praise freely given to the creator. For this reason man may not despise his bodily life. Rather he is obliged to regard his body as good and to hold it in honor since God has created it and will raise it up on the last day. Nevertheless man has been wounded by sin. He finds by experience that his body is in revolt. His very dignity therefore requires that he should glorify God in his body, and not allow it to serve the evil inclinations of his heart. (GS)

We see a strong emphasis on the body and soul as integral to the very dignity of the person. This dignity recognizes material existence but orders it to a divine awareness. This consciousness,

---

[6] *Gaudium et Spes* 1. English translation adapted from *Vatican Council II: Volume 1, The Conciliar and Post Conciliar Documents*, ed. Austin Flannery, O.P. (Northport, NY: Costello Publishing Company, 1996) 903.

this awareness of an ultimate destiny, cannot be ignored or reduced in value without damaging the integrity and dignity of being human. The document continues:

> Man is not deceived when he regards himself as superior to bodily things and as more than just a speck of nature or a nameless unit in the city of man. For by his power to know himself in the depths of his being he rises above the whole universe of mere objects. When he is drawn to think about his real self he turns to those deep recesses of his being where God who probes the heart awaits him, and where he himself decides his own destiny in the sight of God. So when he recognizes in himself a spiritual and immortal soul, he is not being led astray by false imaginings that are due to merely physical or social causes. On the contrary, he grasps what is profoundly true in this matter. (GS 14)

Throughout the documents of Vatican II one senses a similar transposition of the traditional concept of the soul to that notion of the deep recesses of the dignity of the human person. The traditional doctrinal understanding of the soul created by God, as possessing intellectual and volitional capacities, and the importance of bodily physical existence remains. In using personalist concepts the council maintains a humanist optimism, yet in light of the inhuman realities of the twentieth century it sees humanity's "woundedness" as arising from sin. Sin, we should note, is appreciated along the lines of the Catholic Christian Democratic movement that, as we saw, danced between the individualism of the liberal perspective and the kind of locked-in-place traditionalism of the conservatives.

CATHOLIC SOCIAL TEACHING

A climate of Catholic social and political awareness had emerged prior to Vatican II. We see in the Christian Democratic movement a marshaling of Christians in a common effort to address the atheism of the liberal state. Not only had the Christian Democrats involved the faithful in promoting the Christian concerns as citizens, but people were also sensing something of their own democratic relation to the Church. In Catholic circles the fallout of this was the emergence of an involved laity, guided by the clergy, in what has been called "Catholic action." Pius XI in his encyclical *Non Abbiamo Bisogno* (1931) defended a kind of Catholic action intent on improving relations with the governments and reclaiming nonpracticing Catholics. In Belgium the emphasis was on Catholic youth movements, with a simple mission summed up in the slogan "see-judge-act"; and in the United States numerous organizations emerged, some under the control of the local bishops, others more independent. The effect of these movements was to create a very organized network of Catholics with ever increasing political voice in political life. This sense of democratic involvement, guided and encouraged by the Church hierarchy, promoted a spiritual integration that was socially minded and guided by Christian principles. The crucial need for ecclesial guidance characterizes this tradition's point of contention. The Church's tradition of social encyclicals, beginning with *Rerum Novarum* (1891) up to the present, clearly set forth the Church's social concerns. However, after having set in motion an active laity, called to greater participation in Vatican II, the link to magisterial guidance became more critical and more difficult.

The challenge in providing anecdotal illustrations in this tradition is that we meet a flood of popular regional movements. The Catholic Worker movement in America, founded in 1933, promoted the popes' encyclicals on social justice through their newspaper and activities. The twentieth century saw a blossoming of the Catholic press and *l'Osservatore Romano* (est. 1861) reached international distribution. In 1903, the Catholic Daughters of America was founded for "the preservation of the Catholic faith, the intensification of patriotism, the spiritual and intellectual development of Catholic women, and the promotion of charitable projects."[7] The involvement of the laity in Holland,

[7] Richard P. McBrien, Harold W. Attridge, et al., eds., *The HarperCollins Encyclopedia of Catholicism* (New York: HarperCollins, 1995) 256.

as a kind of fifth column, especially in matters of social teaching, created a style of social-critical spiritual integration conducive to the Church's political interest and the climate of the time. However, a potential for rebellion existed from this involved laity, especially concerning the Church's magisterial guidance. The relation of such Catholic action movements to the Church and the institutional Church's attitude toward them are instructive and can be seen in the encyclicals of recent popes.

PAPAL ENCYCLICALS

Pope John XXIII, Paul VI, and John Paul II have promoted a kind of loyalist Catholicism that took seriously their magisterial role. These popes, especially through their encyclicals, addressed the social realities, appealing to the involvement of individuals. John XXIII's *Mater et Magistra* (1961) looked at the social conditions in light of Catholic teaching. In giving his reason for this encyclical he appealed to all people of goodwill:

> We are aware of Our responsibility to take up this torch which our predecessor [Leo XIII] lighted, and hand it on with undiminished flame. It is a torch to lighten the pathways of all who would seek appropriate solutions to the many social problems of our times. (50)

He continues, calling on the "personal initiative of private citizens" to promote economic social progress. Here he appeals to Pius XI's "principal of subsidiarity" (see *Quadragesimo Anno* 23, 1931):

> It is an injustice, a grave evil and a disturbance of right order, for a larger and higher association to arrogate to itself functions which can be performed efficiently by smaller and lower societies. (53)

Mater et Magistra promoted a spiritual integration of political and social involvement, and a sense of "home front" missions in its notion of subsidiarity.

Paul VI's *Populorum Progressio* (1967) clearly casts the Church in a role as knowledgeable in human affairs yet respectful of the Modern state:

> However, local and individual undertakings are no longer enough, the present situation of the world demands concerted action based on a clear vision of all economic, social, cultural and spiritual aspects. Experienced in human affairs, the Church, without attempting to interfere in any way in the politics of States, "wants one thing only" led by the Holy Spirit to carry on the work of Christ, who came into this world to witness to the truth—to save, not to judge, to serve, not to be served. (13)

After justifying the Church's participation in modern political discourse, the encyclical next focuses on the Church's mission:

> Founded to establish on earth the kingdom of Heaven and not to conquer any earthly power, the Church clearly states that the two realms are distinct, just as the two powers, ecclesiastical and civil, are supreme, each in its own domain. But since the Church lives in history, she ought to "examine the signs of the times and interpret them in light of the Gospel." Sharing the noblest aspirations of men and suffering when she sees them not satisfied, she wishes to help them attain their full flowering, and that is why she offers men what she possesses as her characteristic attribute: a global vision of man and of the human race. (13)

One can clearly see the personalist and Catholic Democratic agenda behind the text, but in *Populorum Progressio* the Church is giving clear magisterial instruction to Christians and non-Christians alike. This doctrinal factor nurtured lay social movements and political action groups. While the popes were giving greater political responsibility to the laity, they were at the same time creating an awareness, especially in the individualist circles, that these same principles of subsidiarity and distinct domains could be applied to the Church as well.

Perhaps this is why John Paul II's *Sollicitudo Rei Socialis* (1987) came out five years shy of the quarter-century anniversary of *Populorum Progressio* and the hundredth anniversary of *Rerum Novarum* (1891). This encyclical indicated John Paul II's concern for the social climate in the late eighties.[8] *Sollicitudo Rei* addressed in a cautious tone social doctrine, economic development, and evangelization. This encyclical, unlike *Mater et Magistra* and *Populorum Progressio*, established its relation to the previous social encyclicals and their collectively comprising a magisterial corpus:

> The Popes have not failed to throw fresh light by means of those [encyclical] messages upon new aspects of the social doctrine of the Church. As a result, this doctrine, beginning with the outstanding contribution of Leo XIII and enriched by the successive contributions of the Magisterium, has now become an updated doctrinal "corpus." It builds up gradually, as the Church, in the fullness of the word revealed by Christ Jesus and with the assistance of the Holy Spirit, reads events as they unfold in the course of history. She thus seeks to lead people to respond, with the support also of rational reflection and of the human sciences, to their vocation as responsible builders of earthly society. (1.2)

John Paul II's encyclical is clearly magisterial and sought to provide doctrinal guidance in the midst of what the documents call "notable changes" of the last twenty years, and "totally new aspects" (4.2). He goes on, appealing as he says:

> At stake is the dignity of the human person, whose defense and promotion have been entrusted to us by the Creator, and to whom the men and women at every moment of history are strictly and responsibly in debt. As many people are already more or less clearly aware, the present situation does not seem to correspond to this dignity. Every individual is called upon

---

[8] *Centesimus Annus* did in fact mark the hundredth anniversary in 1991.

to play his or her part in this peaceful campaign, a campaign
to be conducted by means, in order to secure development in
peace, in order to safeguard nature itself and the world about
us. The Church too feels profoundly involved in this enterprise, and she hopes for its ultimate success. (47.4)

In his many encyclicals John Paul II expressed a concern not only
for Catholic involvement in the realities of social and political
life, but he also stated quite clearly the Catholic principles to be
held. He was a personalist, in a certain sense, and in that tradition he advocated a slow and organic evolution. My sense is that
his alarm is with the individualism of the liberal state, the materialism and consumerism it entails. Unfortunately, the success
that the Catholic Church has had in Catholic social and political
involvement did not foresee it turning inward on ecclesial
society.

The social political integration of this tradition faces a twofold
shift. The Humanist cosmology of the previous context and the
Church's effort to enter political life may have moved the Christian so far into "the world" that presently we see two forms of
anthropology. On the one hand, the human person is *individualist*
and fosters a political social integration guided by Humanist
principles of the liberal state. On the other hand, the human
person is *personalist* and fosters a political social integration
guided by the relational solidarity of the community, be that
ecclesial community or some other "community." The Church
is working, slowly but organically I believe, toward this second
anthropology. No longer is she able to presume that the laity
provide the "fifth column" in secular affairs. This social-critical
tradition requires a cosmology of solidarity, and for most people
we assign that solidarity to sectarian political causes, liberal or
conservative, inclusive or exclusive, environment or progress,
welfare or work, etc. This doctrinal factor confronts an overly
one-sided cosmology. The Church is evolving toward a (small c)
catholic cosmology as she faces the challenges and scandals from
within, regrettably, somewhat of her own making. What this

means is that this epoch has fostered a Catholic activism in the state and elsewhere that now has turned in on the Church, activism against the genuine injustice in the Church. The encyclical *Veritatis Splendor* (1993) attempted to address this ecclesial deconstruction:

> While exchanges and conflicts of opinion may constitute normal expressions of public life in a representative democracy, moral teaching certainly cannot depend simply upon respect for a process; indeed, it is in no way established by following the rules and deliberative procedures typical of a democracy. Dissent, in the form of carefully orchestrated protests and polemics carried on in the media, is opposed to ecclesial communion and to a correct understanding of the hierarchical constitution of the People of God. Opposition to the teaching of the Church's Pastors cannot be seen as a legitimate expression either of Christian freedom or of the diversity of the Spirits gifts. When this happens, the Church's Pastors have the duty to act in conformity with their apostolic mission, insisting that the right of the faithful to receive Catholic doctrine in its purity and integrity must always be respected. (113.2)

We see that strong magisterial teaching shapes this approach to spirituality. Yet the tension between individualism and personalism can give rise to a vacillation between isolation and solidarity.

Conclusion

This social-critical life context encounters spirituality in the midst of countervailing realities born of a changing world order. Christianity came to terms with the Humanist current of Modernity, but faced the consequences of an immanentist reduction of God. Solidarity, or the "common good," serves as the Catholic corrective to this spirituality, preventing it from selfishly turning into ego-centeredness. In Vatican II the use of *Dignitatis Humanae* transposed the traditional language on the soul, turning it into an acceptable anthropology for the Humanist. The caution that must be maintained is that the purpose of *Dignitatis Humanae* was to subvert self-centered autonomy by an evangelizing solidarity that sought the ultimate end of human existence revealed in Christ. This social-critical spirituality is by far the riskiest of all spiritualities because the previous distinctions between the divine and the human, the sacred and the secular, the transcendent and the immanent are all blurred. Self-help programs, support groups, and psychological counseling are blended with Ignatian exercises, prayer groups, physical disciplines like yoga, and spiritual direction.

I can't help but note a sense of irony in this tradition. Social-critical integration clearly succeeds on the side of Catholic action for the Gospel; however, the problem seems to be among those who have now opted for the individualism of the liberal state. How does one ensure this right of the faithful to receive Catholic doctrine in its "purity and integrity"? Not only that, but a discriminating laity, schooled in political and commercial choice, is prone to question where this "pure" doctrine is to be found. Whether it is Opus Dei, Mother Angelica, NOW, *The Tablet*, or Call To Action, the "Catholic doctrine" in its purity and integrity seems to have multiple vendors. Consequently this tradition, in its Humanist/personalist dimension, is so intimately tied to the self factors of transcendence and integration that it may take the doctrine of redemption (notions of damnation and salvation) to fully integrate doctrine and life. In other words, this spiritual tradition now faces questions of personal integration and transcendence, of one's relatedness as Church and one's dislocation in alterity.

Part III

Conclusion

Significantly, the Synod Fathers stated that "the Christian faithful need a fuller understanding of the relationship between the Eucharist and their daily lives. Eucharistic spirituality is not just participation in Mass and devotion to the Blessed Sacrament. It embraces the whole of life." This observation is particularly insightful, given our situation today. It must be acknowledged that one of the most serious effects of the secularization just mentioned is that it has relegated the Christian faith to the margins of life as if it were irrelevant to everyday affairs. The futility of this way of living—"as if God did not exist"—is now evident to everyone. Today there is a need to rediscover that Jesus Christ is not just a private conviction or an abstract idea, but a real person, whose becoming part of human history is capable of renewing the life of every man and woman. Hence the Eucharist, as the source and summit of the Church's life and mission, must be translated into spirituality, into a life lived "according to the Spirit" (Rom 8:4ff.; cf. Gal 5:16, 25). It is significant that Saint Paul, in the passage of the Letter to the Romans where he invites his hearers to offer the new spiritual worship, also speaks of the need for a change in their way of living and thinking: "Do not be conformed to this world but be transformed by the renewal of your mind, that you may prove what is the will of God, what is good and acceptable and perfect" (12:2). In this way the Apostle of the Gentiles emphasizes the link between true spiritual worship and the need for a new way of understanding and living one's life. An integral part of the eucharistic form of the Christian life is a new way of thinking, "so that we may no longer be children tossed to and fro and carried about with every wind of doctrine" (Eph 4:14).

Pope Benedict XVI
Sacramentum Caritatis 77

Chapter Eight

The Study of Spirituality:
Do You Love Me? Feed My Sheep

   In treating the topic of spirituality, it is evident that I have not
approached it from the perspective of pious practice or devotional prayer, but rather from an animating perspective, something that feeds the human hunger for God. Most important, it
is an approach that studies spirituality as a *locus theologicus*. It
is a place where theology is done, a place where doctrine and
life come together. As we study various spiritual authors, the
guiding question ought to be, How does this particular spiritual
writer bring together a body of beliefs (doctrine) for the person
in a particular historical, social, cultural setting (life)? In the
treatment of Catholic spirituality I identified various traditions
born out of particular life contexts; this explores the questions
of cosmology and anthropology. What is critical is that we also
see how Catholic doctrines met this life context with an integrating sense of creation and redemption. This approach recognizes
the significance in spirituality of religious commitment to a body
of beliefs, and dedication to the community that embodies these

beliefs. "No man is an island, entire of itself; every man is a piece of the continent," as the poet John Donne said, and no spirituality is meant to be idiosyncratic. Consequently, spirituality necessarily requires a religious body that provides magisterial instruction as to its genuine beliefs. Furthermore, each spiritual writer needs to be judged in the context of his or her religious tradition. For example, a Jewish spiritual writer should be read with respect for the Jewish context, a Christian for a Christian context, and so on.

The role of religious tradition in studying spirituality is crucial. Without it, spirituality is reduced to an eclectic and individualized therapy, selfishly intent on "my" well-being. This doctrinal factor is not limited to Christianity, nor is it limited only to the great religious traditions, but cults and communes also function in doctrinal ways, sometimes tragically so. This is why it is of paramount importance that any spirituality be studied and evaluated in light of its doctrinal factors and its framing of the realities underlying the concepts of creation and redemption. These concepts, "how we got here" and "what are we destined to become," serve to safeguard human flourishing and correct a too narrowly defined cosmology and anthropology.

What do I mean by this? In studying various spiritualities it is important that we do not abandon our responsibility to critically evaluate them. Too often works on spirituality avoid any evaluation, critically looking at its strengths and limitations. In asking the questions about a particular spirituality's understanding of the world (cosmology) and of the human person (anthropology) we may look more critically at its sense of human flourishing, human integration. If the world is seen as hostile and the human condition as punishment, we need to challenge its claim to be a proper spirituality. This critical evaluation of its various assumptions helps us to examine a spirituality's notion of how we got here (creation) and where we are headed (redemption). In asking these questions we place spirituality back in its religious context and must evaluate it in light of its theological consistency, or its innovation, or its errors. This allows us to respect the spiritual writer and a particular spirituality as part of the theological enterprise. Spirituality is theology done in a creative and novel way, but it is theology nonetheless.

The Critical Study of Spirituality: Be Transformed by the Renewal of Your Mind

We see that spirituality manifests some key features that have often been ignored by many "spiritual devotees." By examining these three factors (self, life, doctrine) we see that spirituality is first and foremost about an aspect of human existence, the fullness of human existence. It is an existential reality. Life reveals to us that spiritualities emerge because there are new needs so as to better understand an ever-changing world context in which we live. Questions about the world and where the human person belongs in that context demand that spirituality be both theological and moral. In this twofold consideration we more clearly see that spirituality is social and communal. As such it explores two realities: (1) the social structures (temple, synagogue, church, abbey, ashram, anchor, as well as religious and secular institutions); and (2) the social relations (teacher, disciple, friend, neighbor, enemy, persecutor, as well as ecclesial and political interests). Spirituality, no matter how sophisticated, or what denomination or faith, will always manifest a "theology" and a "morality." Spiritualities must be intellectually satisfying and morally desirable; if not, they do not last. Even when it seems lacking, or comes across as too simplistic, the fact is that a spirituality will satisfy both the intellectual and volitional needs of human flourishing. If not, it is hard to see it as a proper spirituality. Why is that? Because in the end, any spirituality must come around to the equivalent doctrinal factors of creation and redemption. These notions are about how any religious tradition understands the divine interaction with the human and its sense of each person's ultimate destiny.

Creation and redemption bring the self, and the reality of one's life, into a peculiar integration of human existence. For the person it is the human encounter with absolutely transcendent otherness. Particular religious traditions will be the first to condemn its false spiritualities, but a true spirituality does something profound to a particular religious tradition. A true spirituality brings together a myriad of factors long forgotten or taken for granted, and breathes new life, animating the tradition itself. In the critical study of spirituality, one must examine the life and person of particular writers, but it is with the introduction of its doctrines that life and person are refocused. This is why a study of Christian spirituality, which we have undertaken, needs to examine Christian doctrine and the specific spirituality of a person appreciated in light of its animating both doctrine and life. In the preceding chapters I have suggested four "traditions" of Christian, and specifically Catholic, spiritual integration: ascetical, mystical, aesthetical, and social-critical. My purpose has been to demonstrate that self and life are animated by doctrine. This animation is fundamental to a Christian anthropology and to the animation of Catholic doctrine and Christian life. In each "tradition" we see that particular historical and social realities, the cosmology, give rise to questions that require magisterial instruction. In this work we could only offer illustrations of this method. However, the study of spiritual integration must respect the specific fact of a person, in a time and a place, animating doctrine and life. As helpful as identifying "schools of spirituality" can be, it ought to suggest rather than define an approach to spiritual integration. Asceticism, mysticism, aestheticism, and social-criticalism are helpful tools in examining a spiritual work but the labels ought not to exhaust the spiritual animation of an author. There is more in a particular spirituality than such labels name; there is the animation of doctrine in one life, a lived theological reality.

With that caution I risk oversimplifying spirituality by offering the following table. Please realize it is meant to give the reader a "thumbnail" of the reality. As helpful as it may seem, it is also harmful if taken as a reduction of all that has gone before.

Spiritual Tradition	Cosmology	Implied Anthropology	Key Doctrine	Spiritual Integration Creation/Redemption
Ascetical Approach	The world context is one of a dualistic battle between good and evil, light and dark.	Life is struggle, a battle that is to be won by austere sacrifice.	**Christology** The nature and person of Christ.	Jesus shows us how to live in this life so as to win the victor's crown in the life to come.
Mystical Approach	The world context is "a world of understanding" that is full of ideas and imagination. It is a riddle that we discover.	Life is about intellectual delight, the mind's lifting the veil to the world beyond the physical.	**Trinity** The mystery and nature of the Triune God who is, who was, and who will be—who holds the fullness of all that is to be revealed.	By pondering the life of the Trinity we participate in that divine life, a life of grace. God is courting us if we but discover his gifts.
Aesthetical Approach	The world context is marked by the physical, mathematical, material, and scientific, but seeks in the beauty of nature a possible hint of something more. The individual must decide if this is real or myth.	Life is what I make of it. I "am the measure of all things" (Protagoras). "God has placed no limits to the exercise of the intellect he has given us, on this side of the grave" (Sir Francis Bacon). "God's in his heaven; all's right with the world" (unknown origin, quoted by Robert Browning).	**Incarnation** The free act of an all-powerful God to choose to enter into the human condition as one of us.	God is the Supreme author, poet, artist, and has charged all of creation with infinite wonder and beauty. By choosing to enter into this wonder, this beauty, we open ourselves to enter into the will of God.
Social-Critical Approach	The world context is marred by the failure of human ideals and the tyranny of evil, man's inhumanity to man. There is nothing out there and we are all alone.	Life is about my looking after number one, *numero uno*. The "Me" generation. *I'm Good Enough, I'm Smart Enough, and Doggone It, People Like Me! Daily Affirmations by Stuart Smalley* (Al Franken).	**Soteriology** God's plan of salvation. Why would an all-powerful God choose to die and truly share in human suffering? Why did Jesus have to suffer and die?	"For God sent his Son into the world not to judge the world, but so that through him the world might be saved" (John 3:17). The cost of our freedom is that we have an unbelievable capacity for evil and yet God's love will not abandon us. Salvation is found in our communal sharing in his redemptive suffering, his passion, death, and resurrection, as the Church, the Body of Christ.

Animating Spirituality

In the study of spirituality it is important to treat a spiritual writer using the factors of doctrine and life. While spiritual writings will no doubt continue to inspire people, for I do not mean to reduce the value of one's own devotional reading, there is something more that is demanded in our studying them. Perhaps it is fair to say that great spiritual writers are so, because in their life and writings, they model a kind of human flourishing. Through their integration and sense of transcendence they demonstrate how the human person ought to be related to the cosmos and located in the fullest sense of human existence. True spiritual writers offer us insights to the workings of the world. They manifest the riches of the human vocation—that is, to be religious.

Yes, religious! The human call is one of being linked to the God who calls us into being and who gathers us into one, both our origin and our destiny. The great spiritual writers, of any tradition, help us to see the divine in our midst and to live here and now, mindful of what awaits us. But this is not done in isolation. No, of its very nature, spirituality will constitute community, will draw and link people together; after all, that is what the Latin root *religare* means. In a proper sense, spirituality must be "religion bound" because it is "religiously binding." The truly great spiritual figures have been Abraham, Moses, Jesus, Mohammed, Confucius, Gautama Buddha, and many of the ancient ones forgotten to history, who first bound a people to God. In so doing, all people of faith have journeyed toward a fuller understanding of the human vocation. This is worth restating! People of faith, people who have a desire to see more than meets the eye, and who search to understand its meaning, help us to discover something more to the human project, its spiritual dimension.

If one wishes to respect its integrity, Christian spirituality must be read within the context of Christian doctrine. Furthermore, it seems fair that one also read Catholic, Protestant, or Orthodox spirituality mindful of two things. First, that all such Christian spiritual writers are properly bound to Christ. And second, that each denomination needs to be respected in interpreting its spiritual writings. For that matter, within Catholicism we can further speak of Benedict, Dominic, Francis, and Ignatius (to name a few) as spiritual traditions. Each tradition has its own set of doctrine which ought to be appreciated. In so doing, one's study of these spiritualities will receive the kind of discipline so necessary for reaching into its depths. Psychology shows us that we can speak of religion as "extrinsic" or "intrinsic."[1] In the first, religion is functional and utilitarian, while in the second the person's religion is formative; it shapes the person. While one could debate the polarity, I would say that the spiritual writers and their spiritualities are found within the intrinsic understanding of religion. As such, spirituality is formative of the inner person and this is along religious lines. At the same time we need to allow the doctrines to be read critically. How does this belief foster human flourishing, our ultimate destiny? If we were to deprive the spiritual writer of this intrinsic religious dimension—to take Judaism from Rabbi Isaac Luria; Christianity from Gregory of Nazianzus, or Symeon, or Julian, or Merton; to take Protestantism from Böhme, or Bonhoeffer; Sufism from 'Abd al-Qādir; or Hinduism from Abhinavagupta—their spirituality would be reduced to a philosophical system like socialism or feminism. It is very difficult to see the logic when a person naively says, "Oh, I am spiritual, I'm just not religious." Spiritualities are linked to religion! As distasteful as this may be to some who wrongly see religion as oppressive, it is only in the integrity of religious, communal solidarity that we meet the truth that is bigger than ourselves.

There is something inside us all that hungers for that something more, which can only be found in genuine spirituality. Spirituality is fundamentally about the human, about true humanity. It is about our potentials and possibilities, our limits and

---

[1] A distinction made by psychologists G.W. Allport and J.M. Ross, "Personal Religious Orientation and Prejudice," *Journal of Personality and Social Psychology* 5 (1967): 432–43.

disorders. If we want to do justice to a particular person, we need to examine the reality of his or her time and place—how one's religious tradition animates religious doctrine, brings it to life. History demands that we allow a person's religious context to correctly interpret what may seem to us as odd, wrong, or dysfunctional. As the Native American adage goes, we ought not to judge another person until we've walked a mile in his moccasins. Only then will a particular spirituality be able to function on behalf of the great task of human flourishing. It will confirm what is best in the human project, but, more important, it will also challenge what is destructive in it. Consequently, the study of spirituality must preserve that "lived reality of religion" for the integrity of the spirituality itself. Without it, the unique integration, so valuable to the human project, escapes us. For it is in these spiritualities that some depth of the human person is awakened and a person's life makes sense. As I have already stated, at its best, spirituality in our tradition is an existential animation of Catholic doctrine, which is both intellectually satisfying and morally desirable. Such a spiritual lifestyle rests in the soul's unifying presence that uniquely integrates the vast array of one's human existence. This relating takes place in integration, which is the heart, and soul, of spirituality. Approaching spirituality in this way is truly animating.

Index